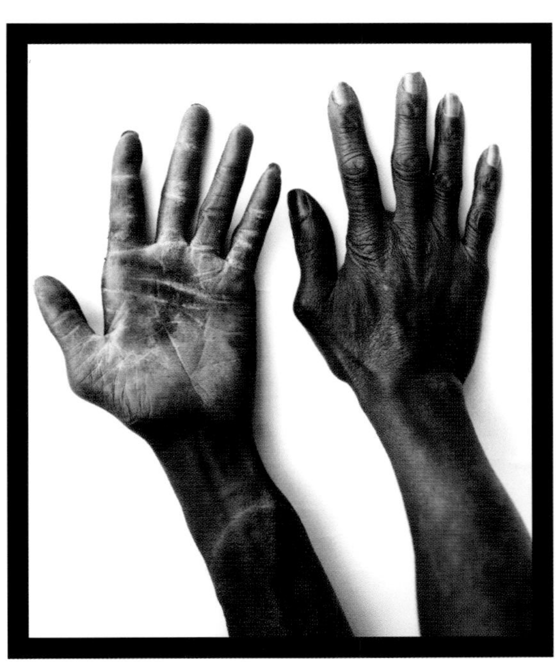

Portraits From the Belly of the Whale by Michael Garlington


First Published 2005



ISBN# 0-9762747-3-6

Book and cover design by Whitney McAtee
Art direction by Jay Blakesberg
All high-resolution scanning and digital file preparation by Paul Halmos
www.paulhalmos.com

Printed by CK Graphics, San Francisco, California

Published by Rock Out Books
P.O.Box 460054
San Francisco, California 94146
www.rockoutbooks.com
email: info@rockoutbooks.com

Distributed by SCB Distributors
15608 S. New Century Drive
Gardena, Ca 90248

310-532-9400

www.scbdistributors.com

to Mark

# PORTRAITS FROM THE BELLY OF THE WHALE

BY MICHAEL GARLINGTON

Greetings from The Belly of the Whale

♥ Mike

*This book is dedicated to*
*my Mother and Amy*

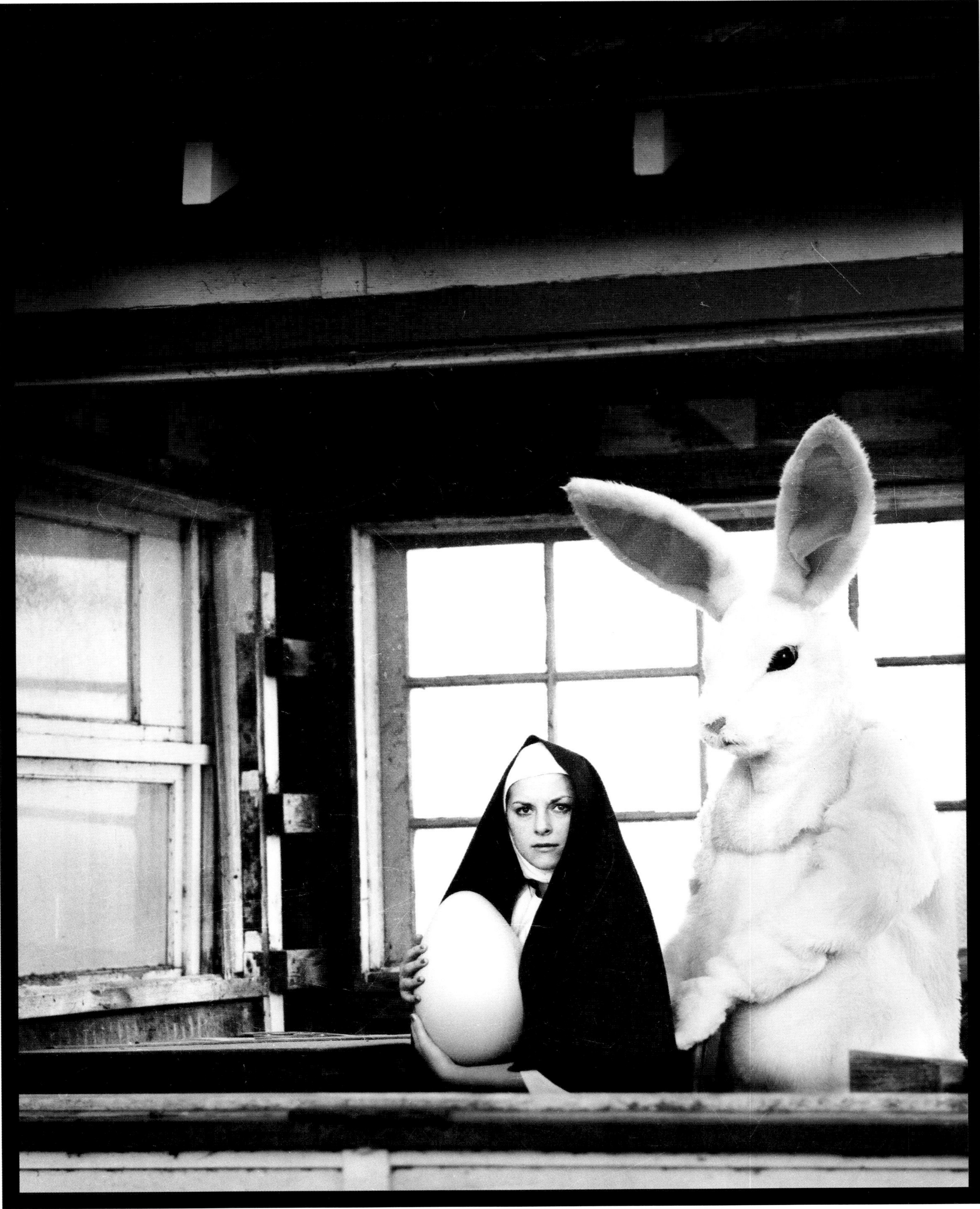

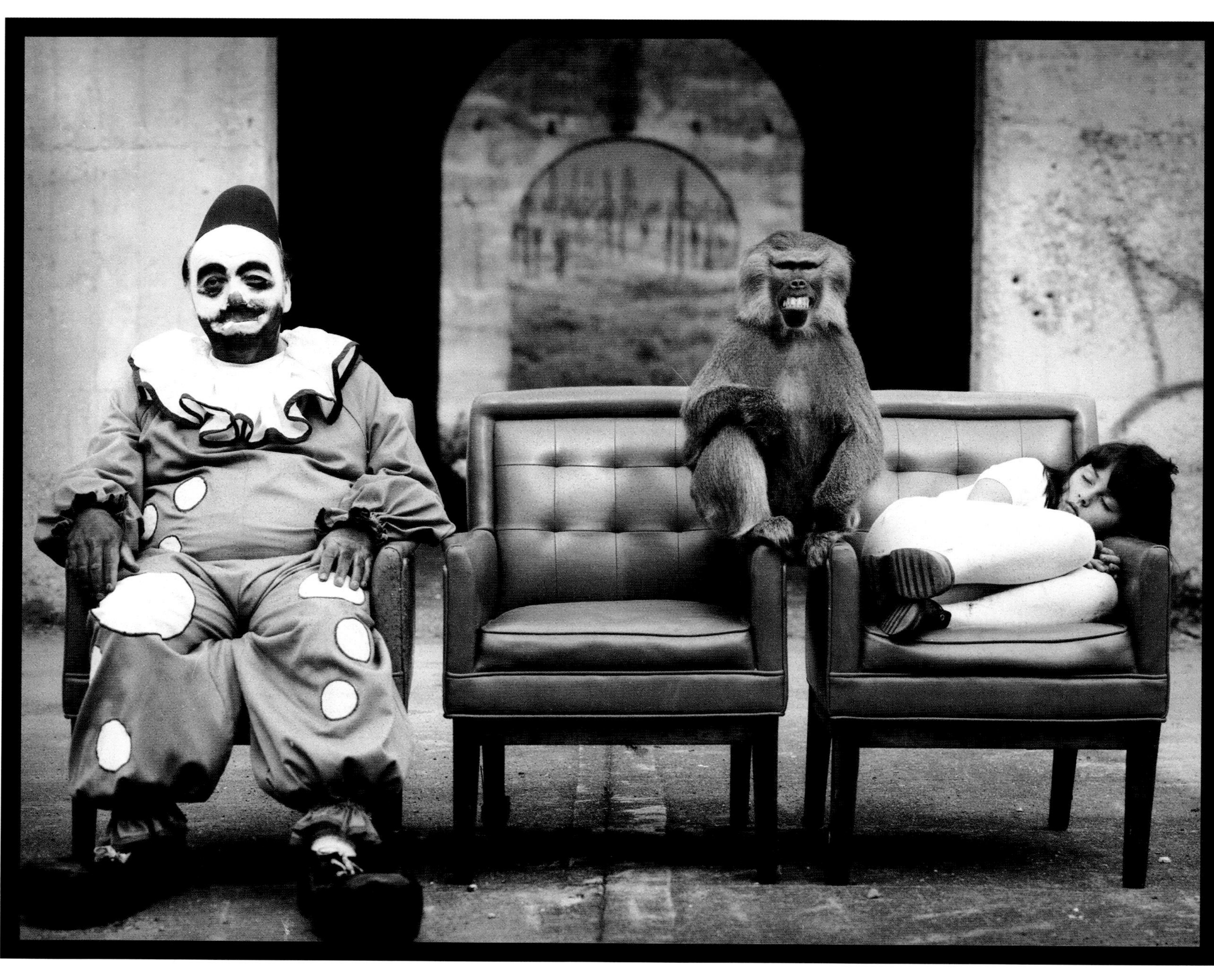

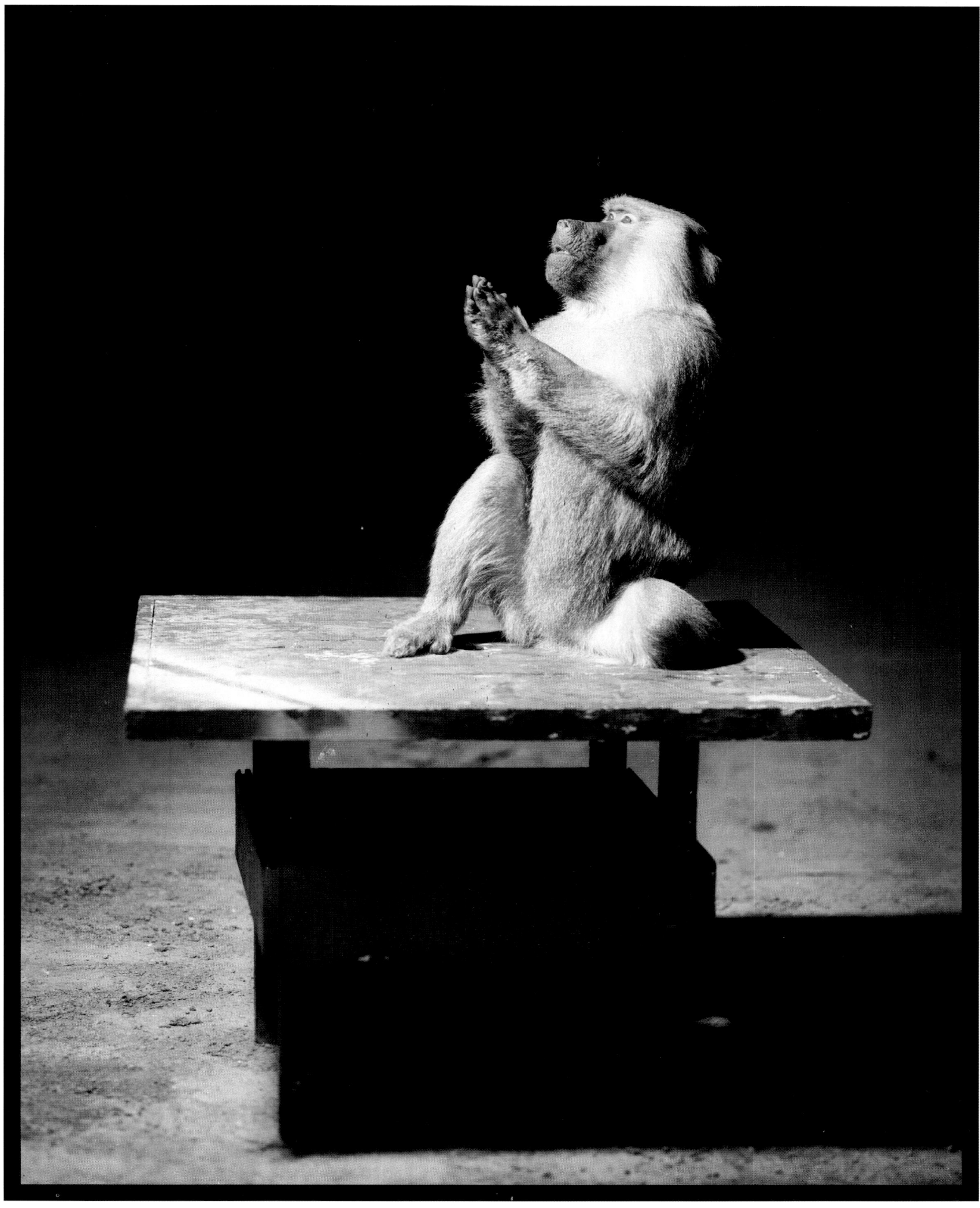

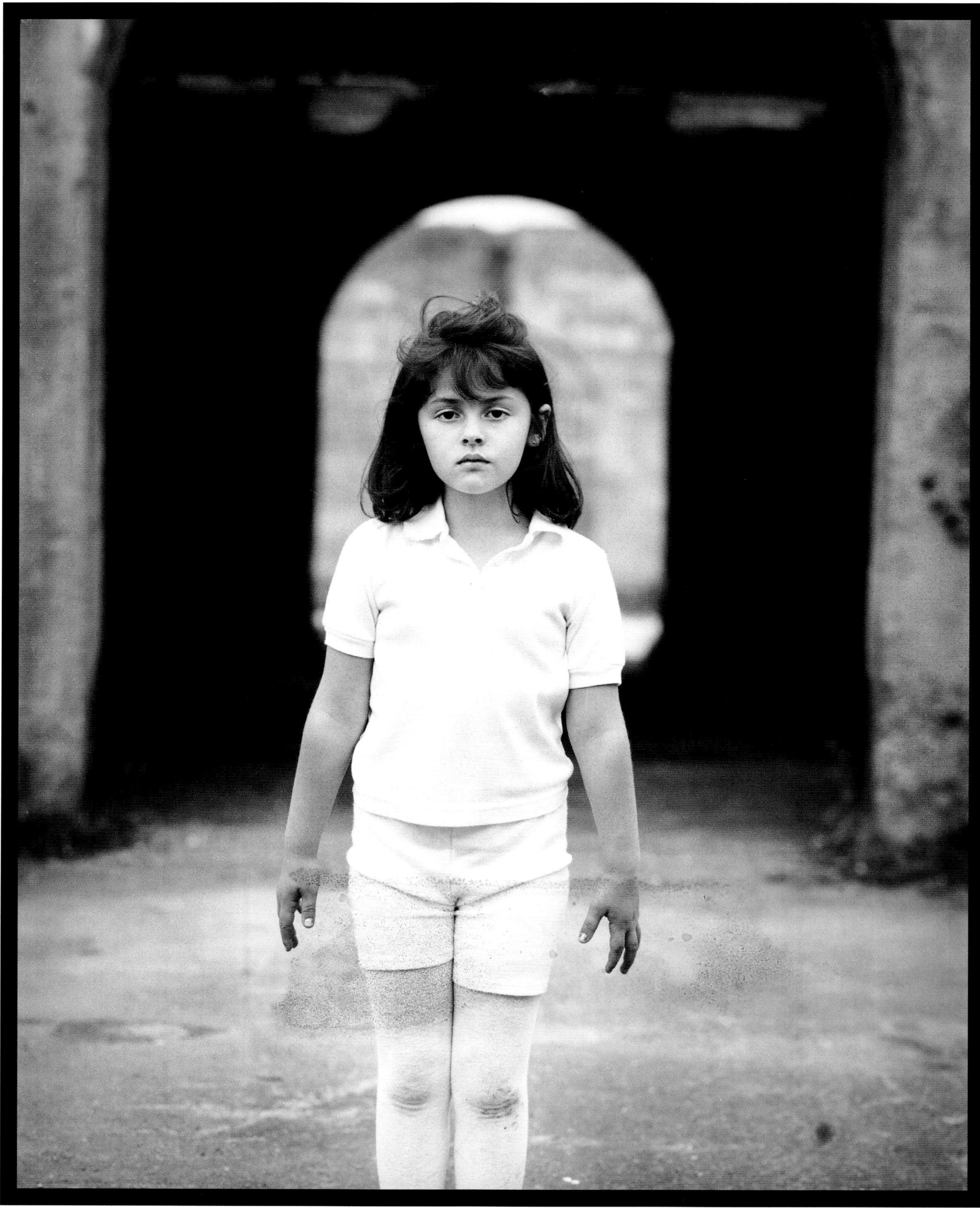

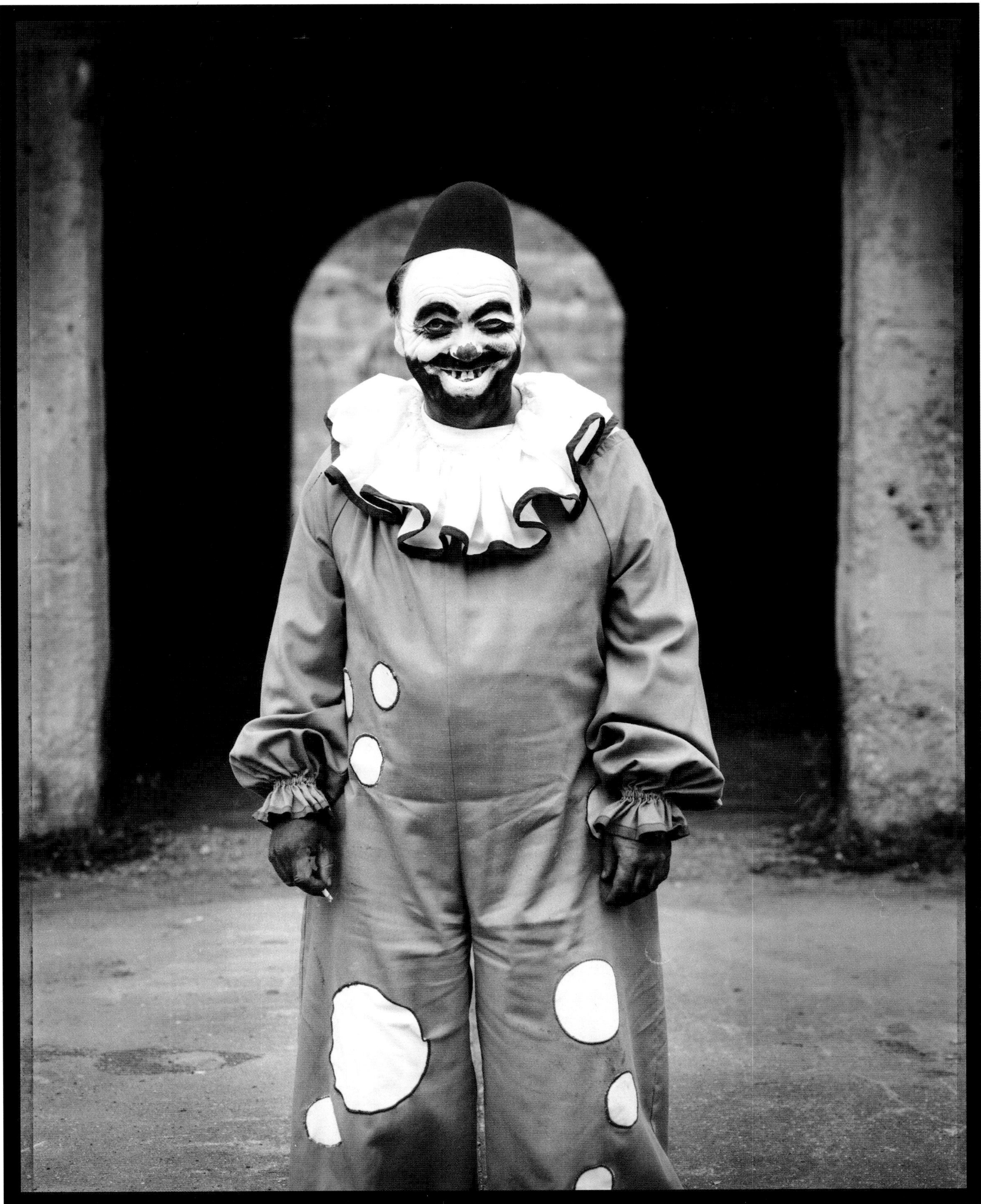

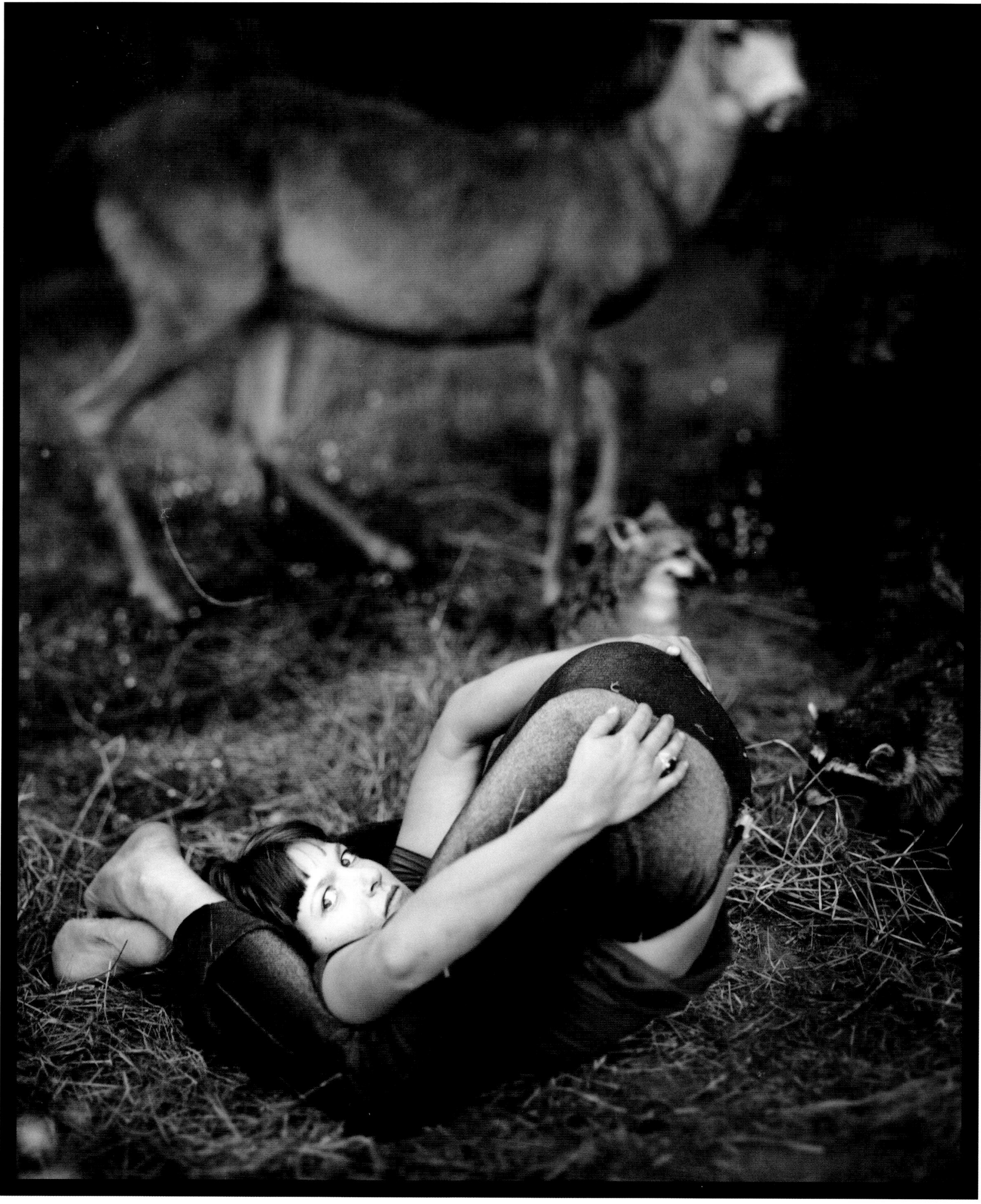

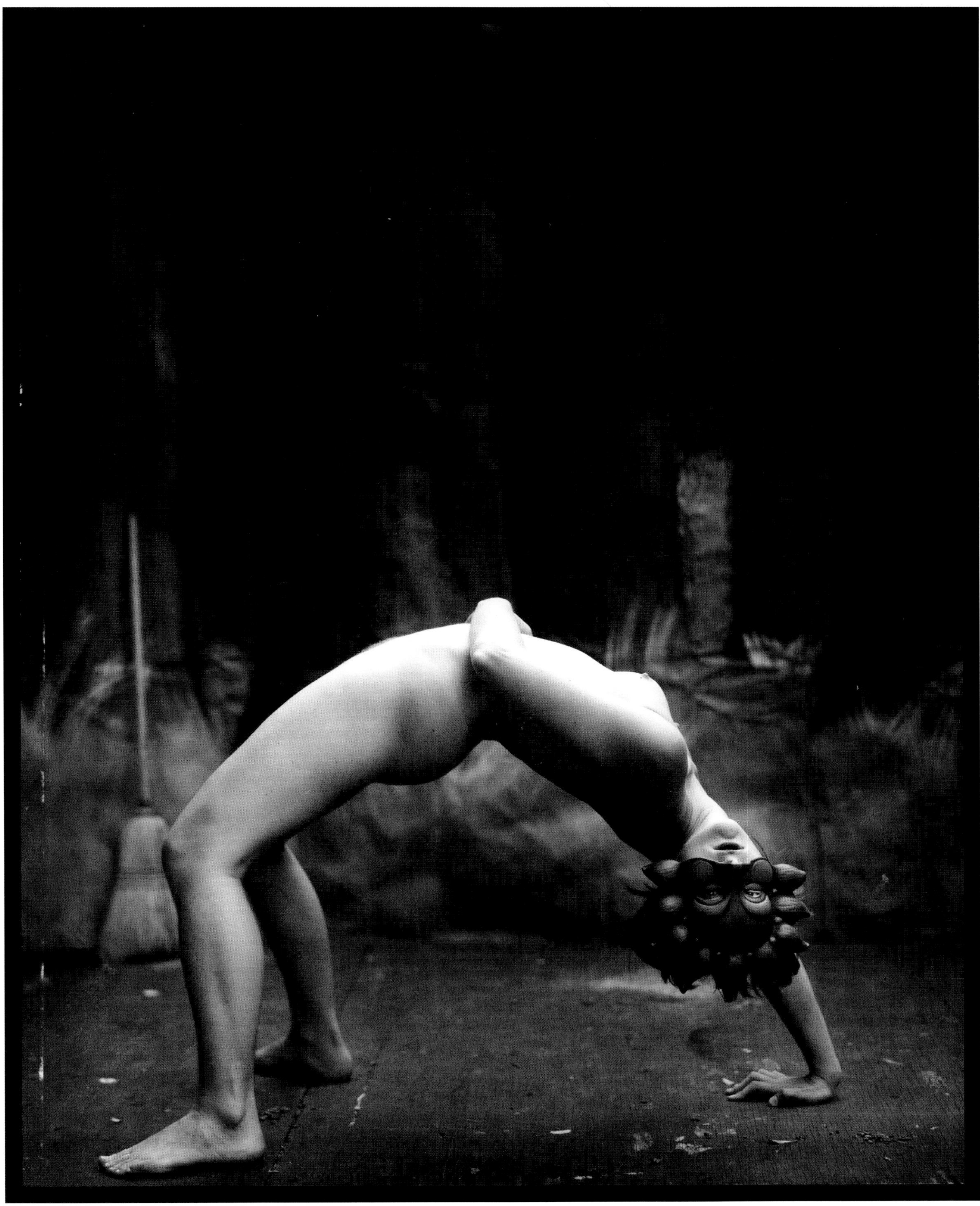

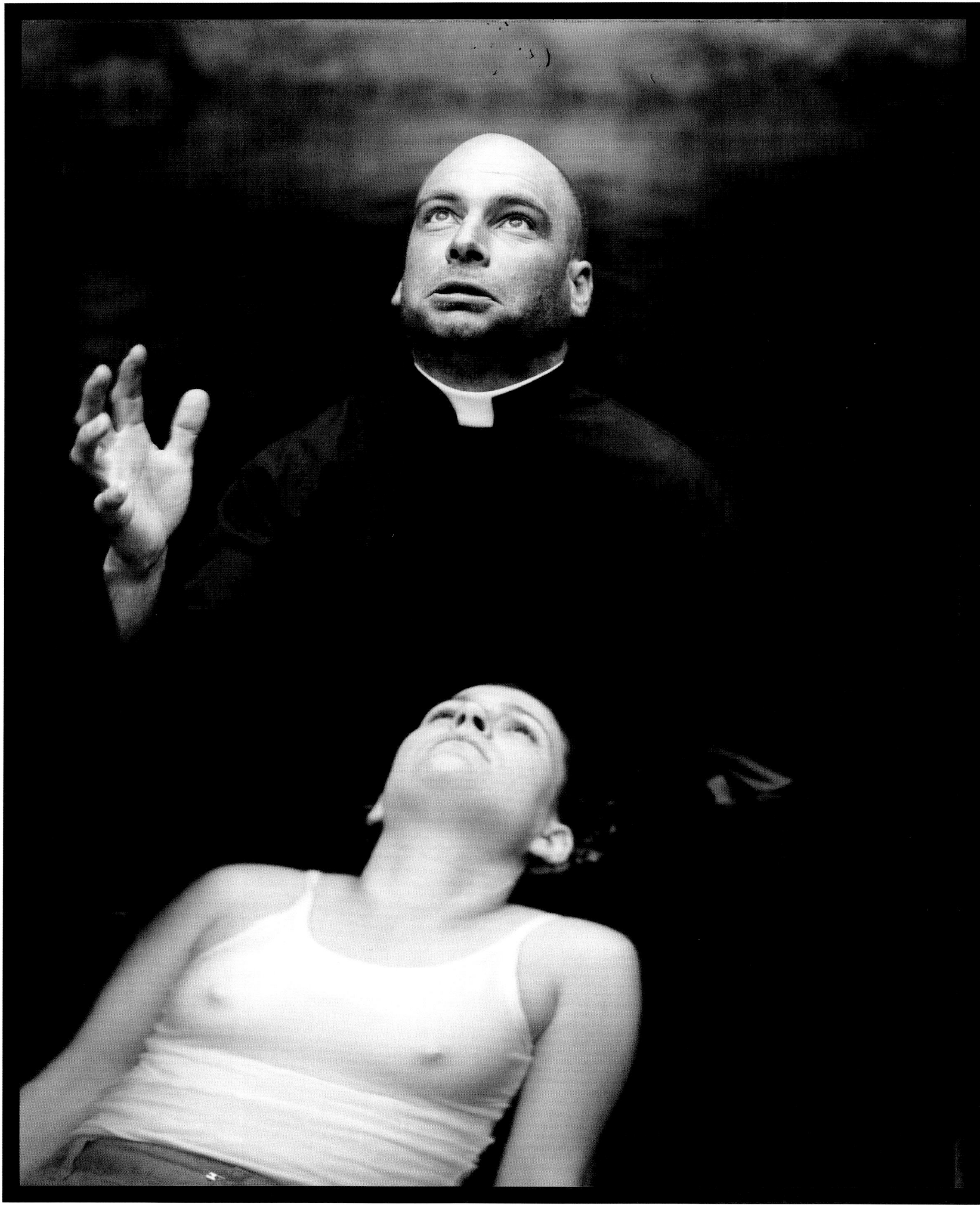

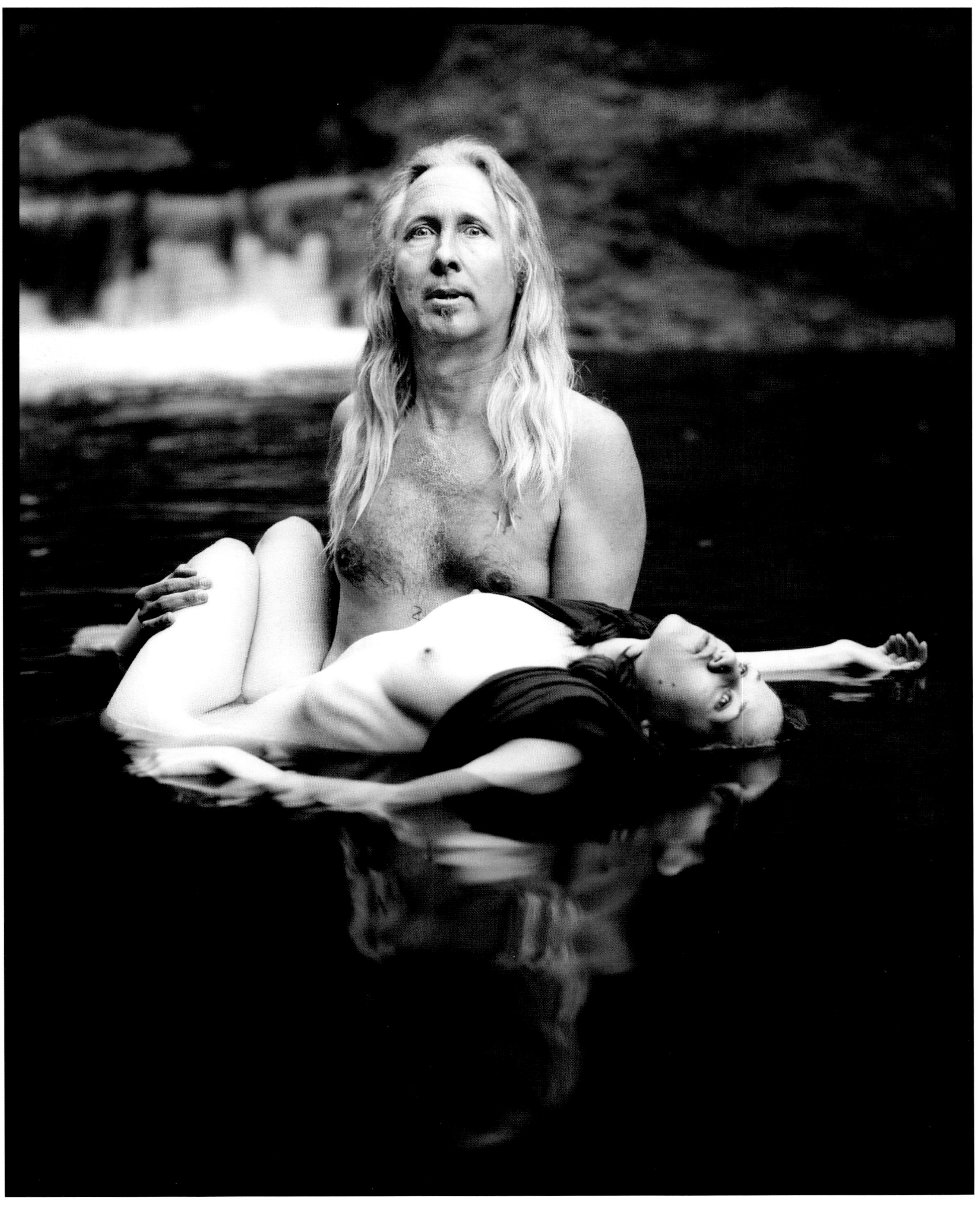

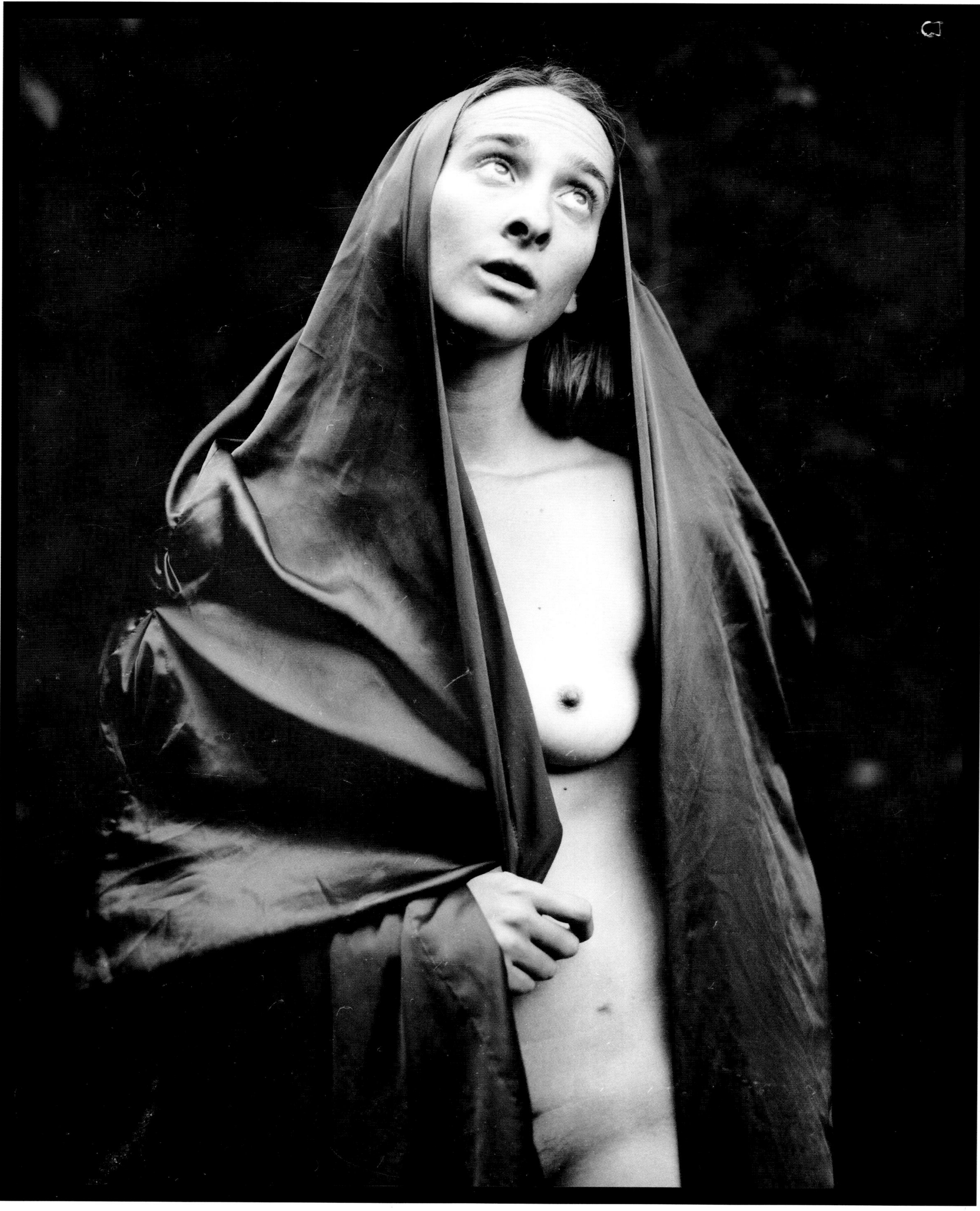

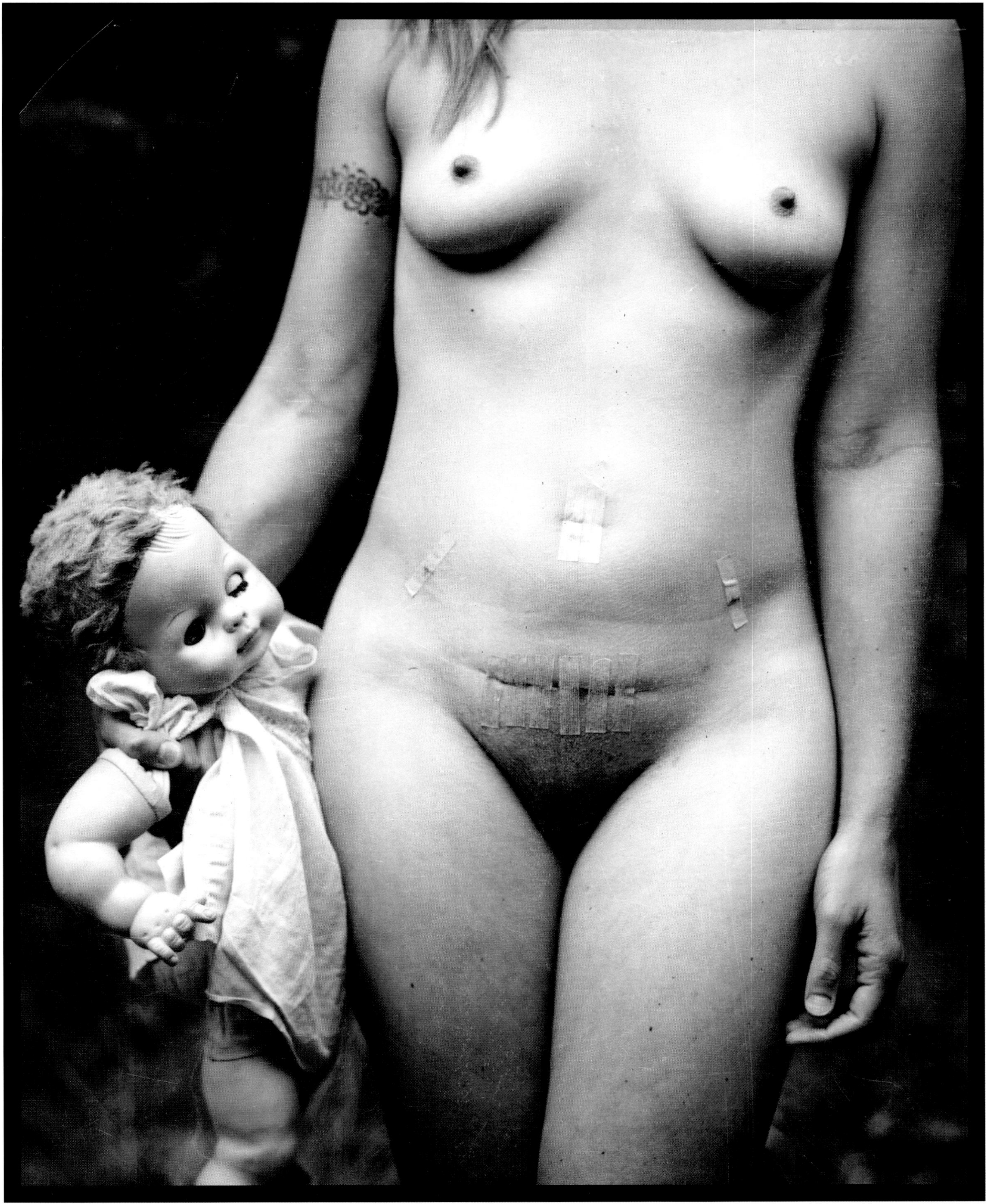

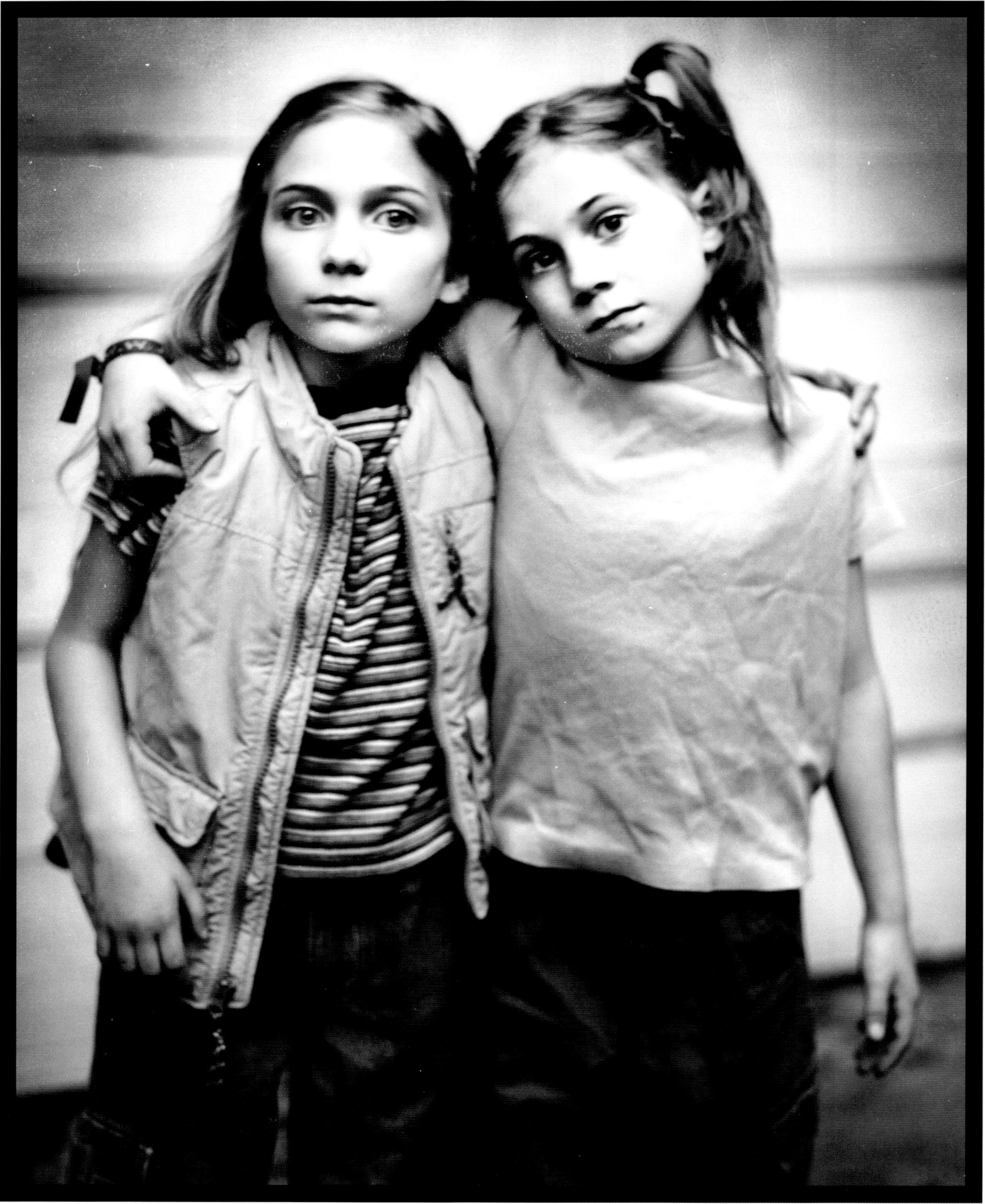

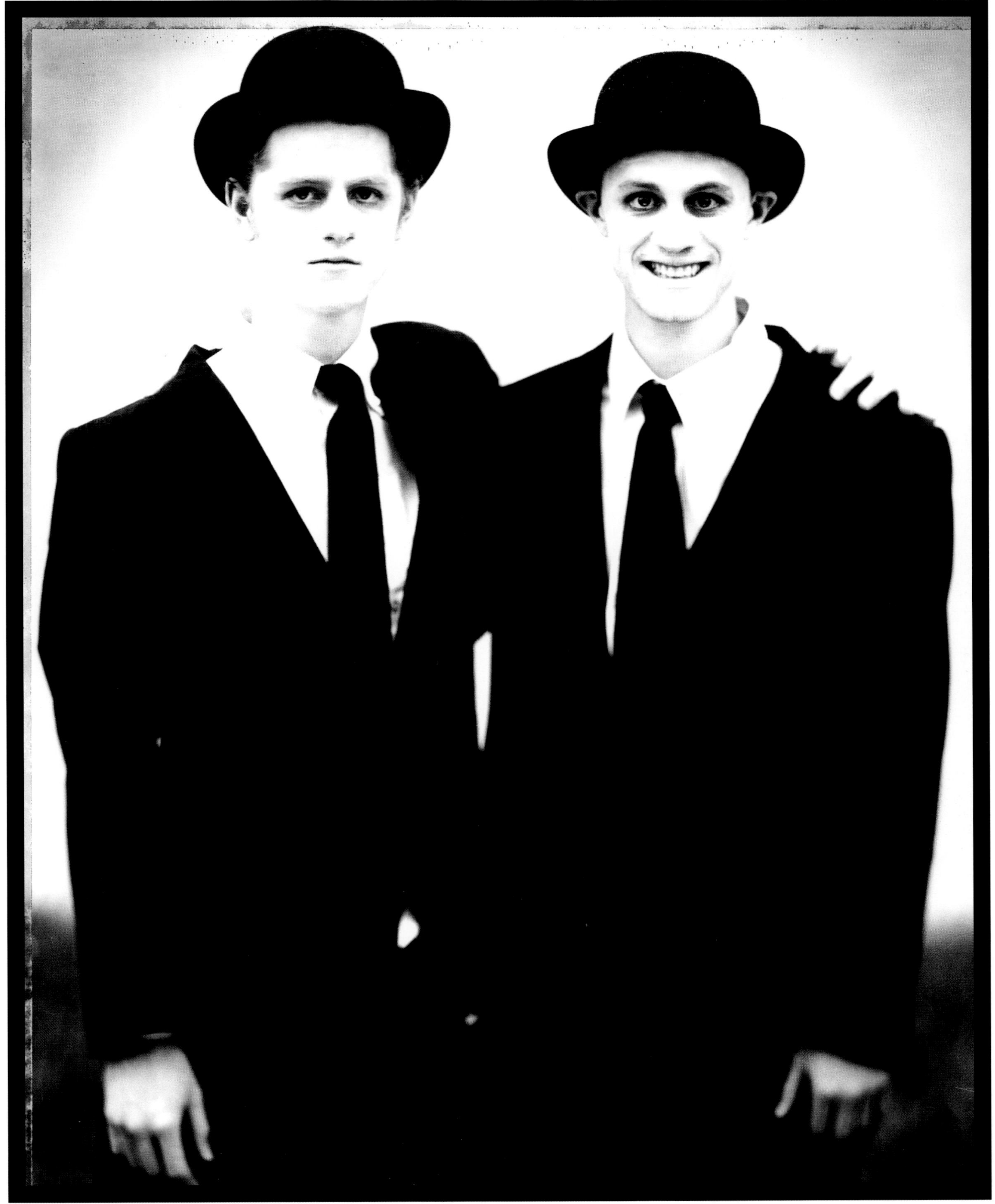

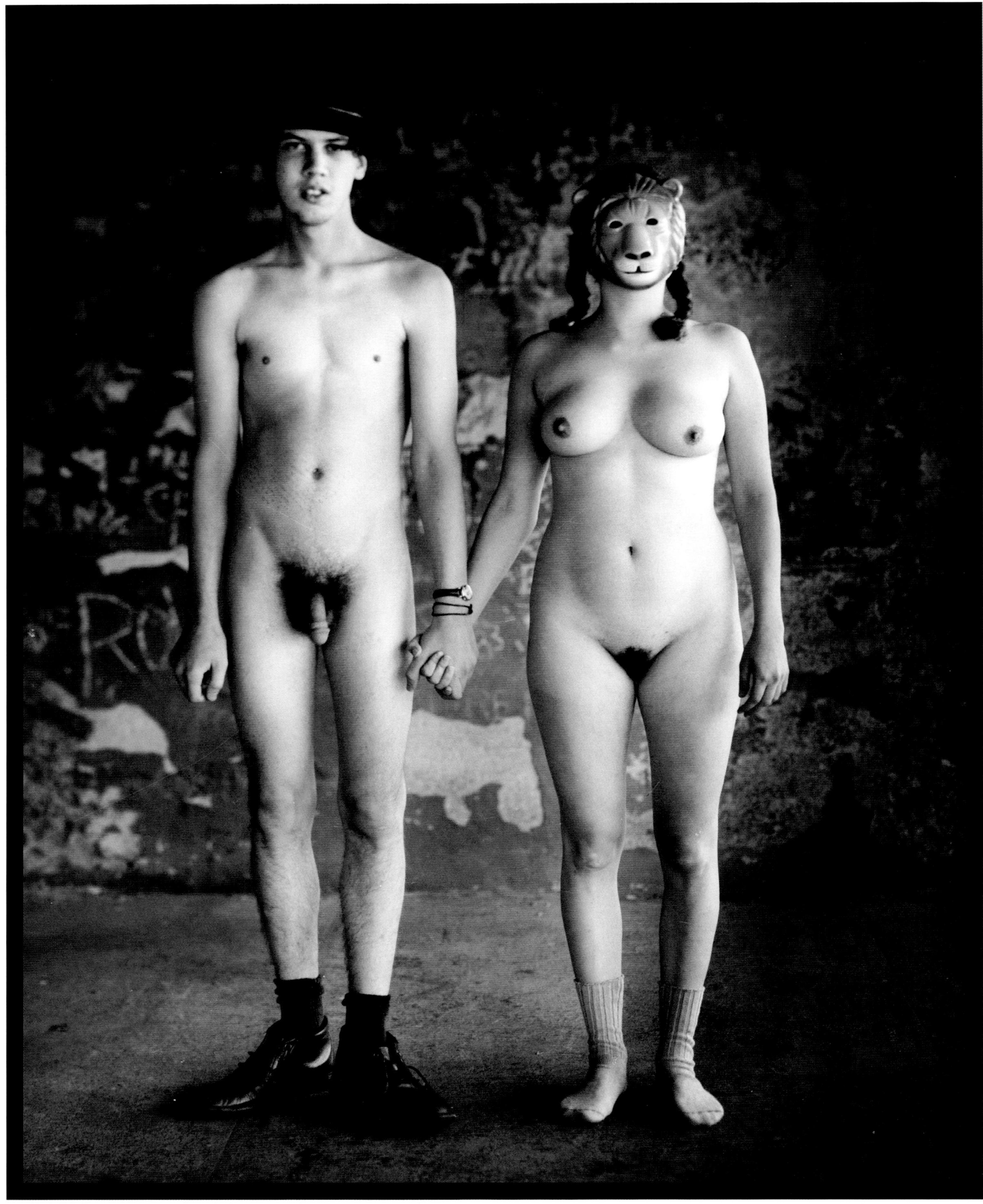

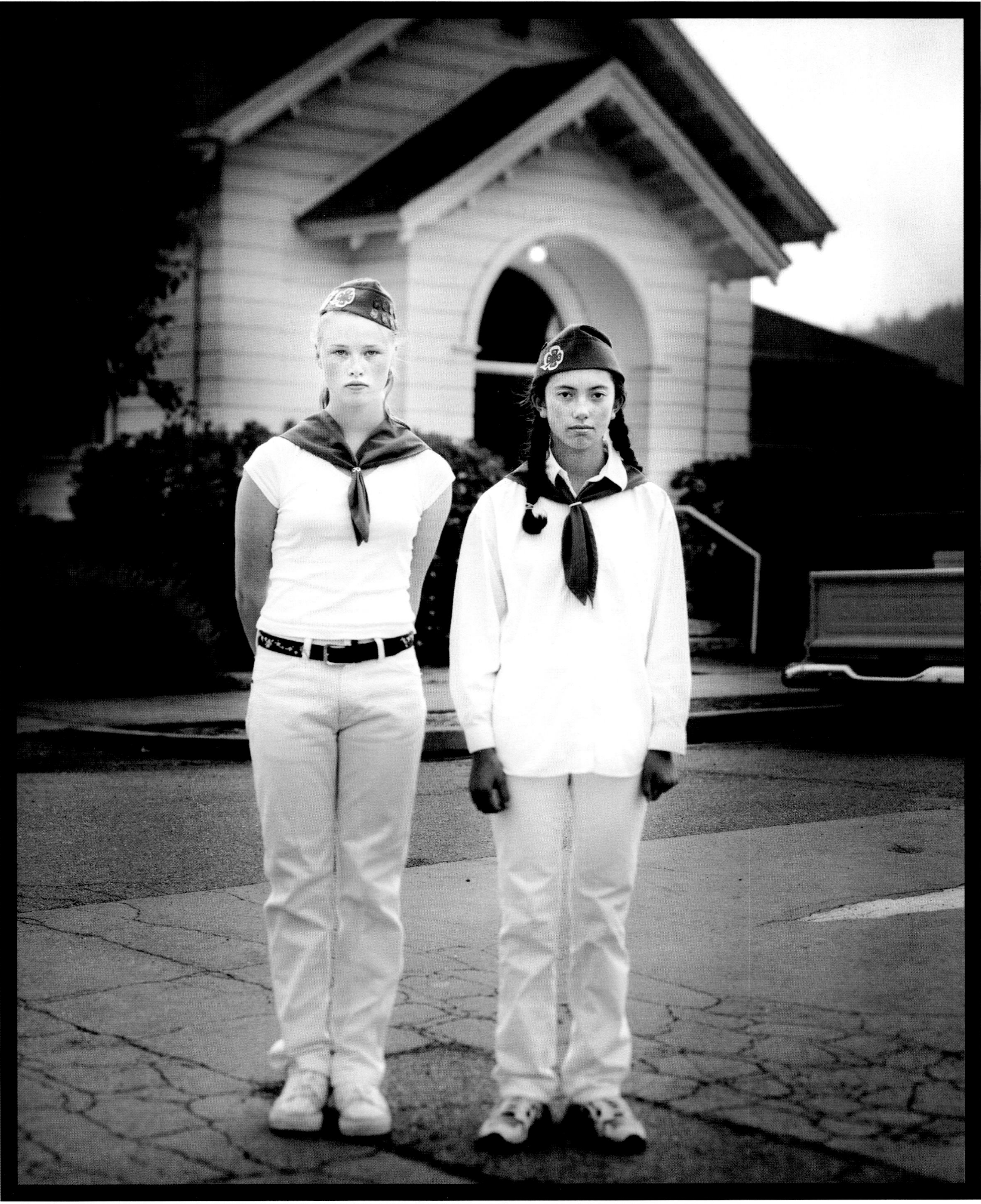

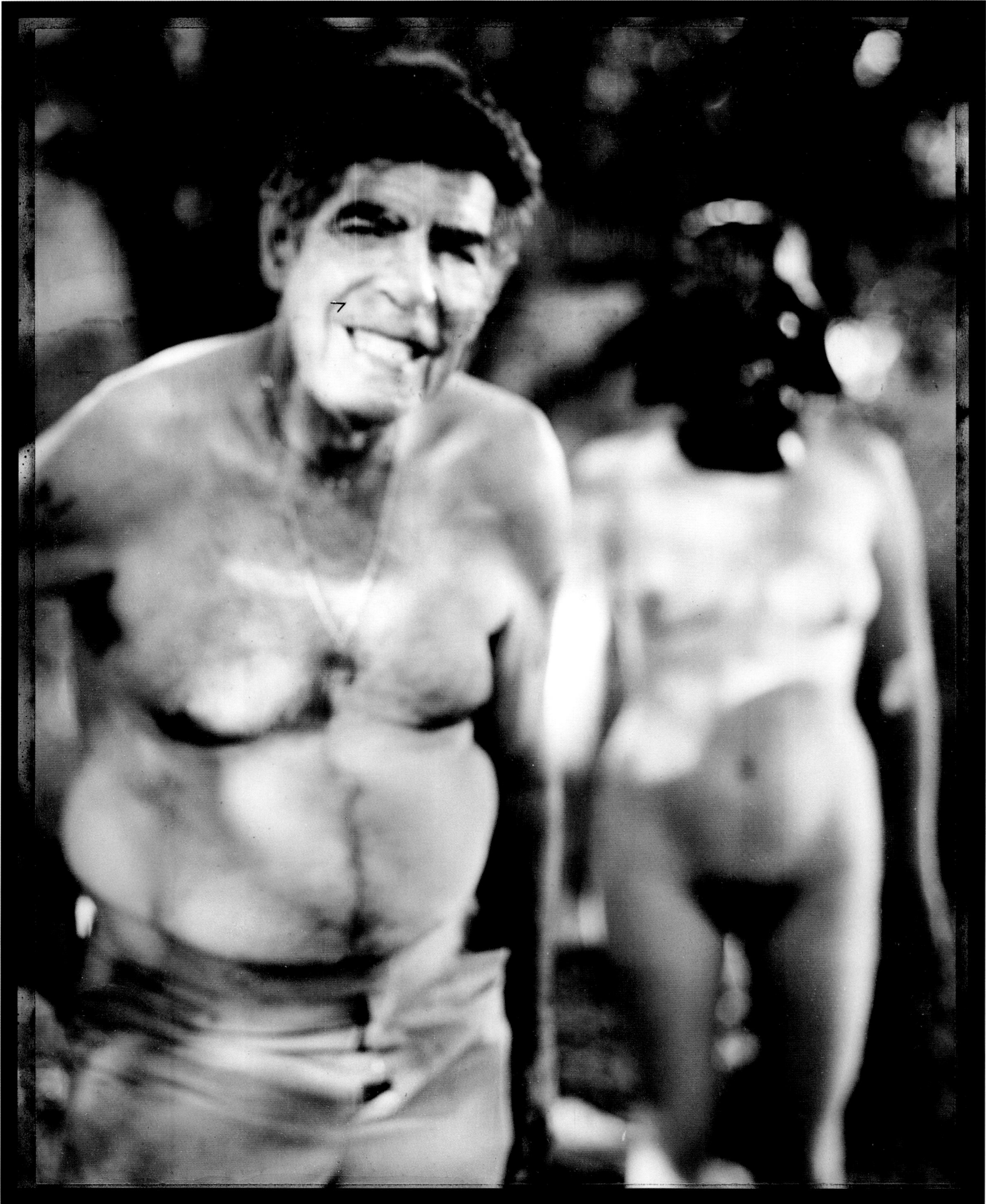

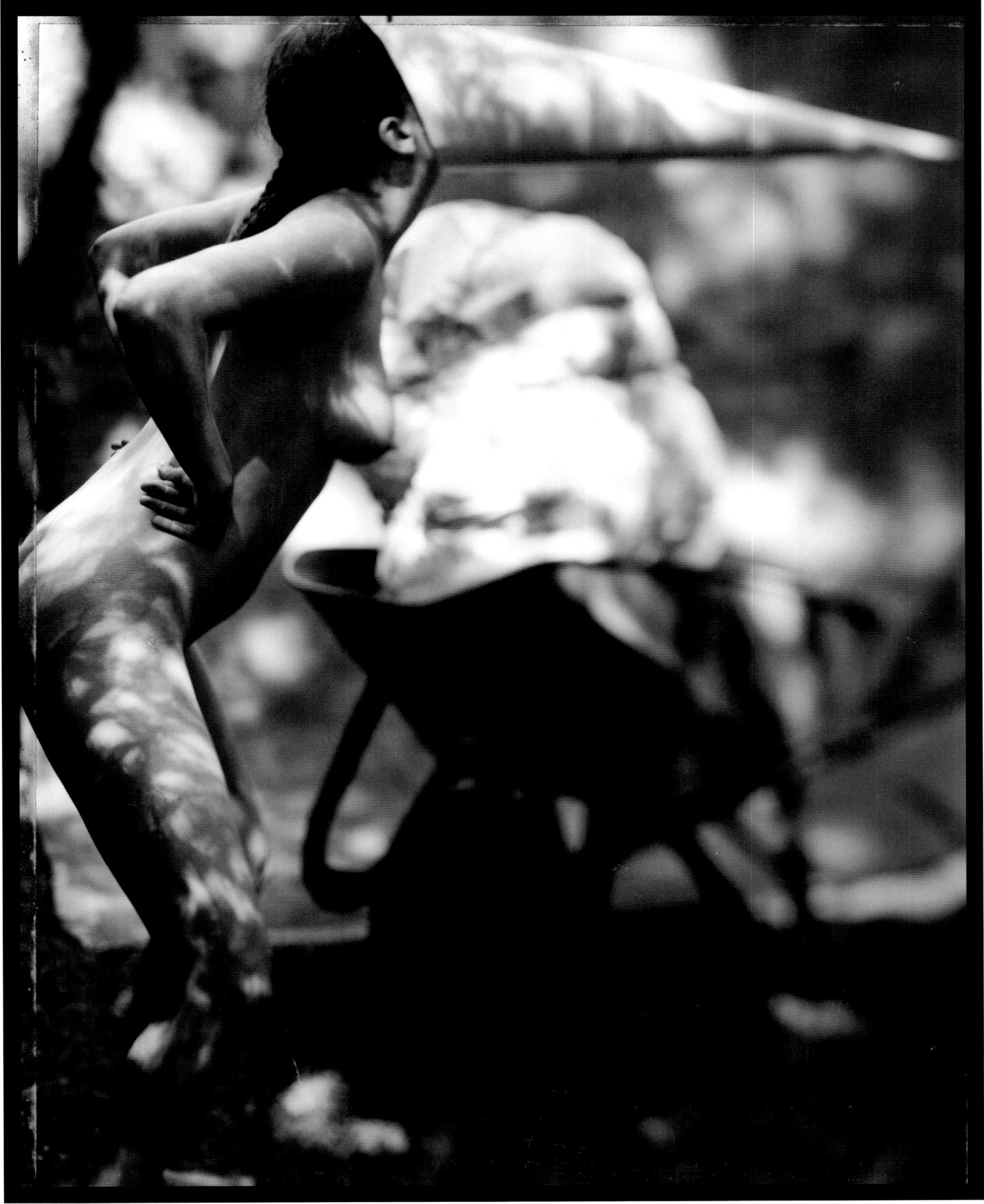

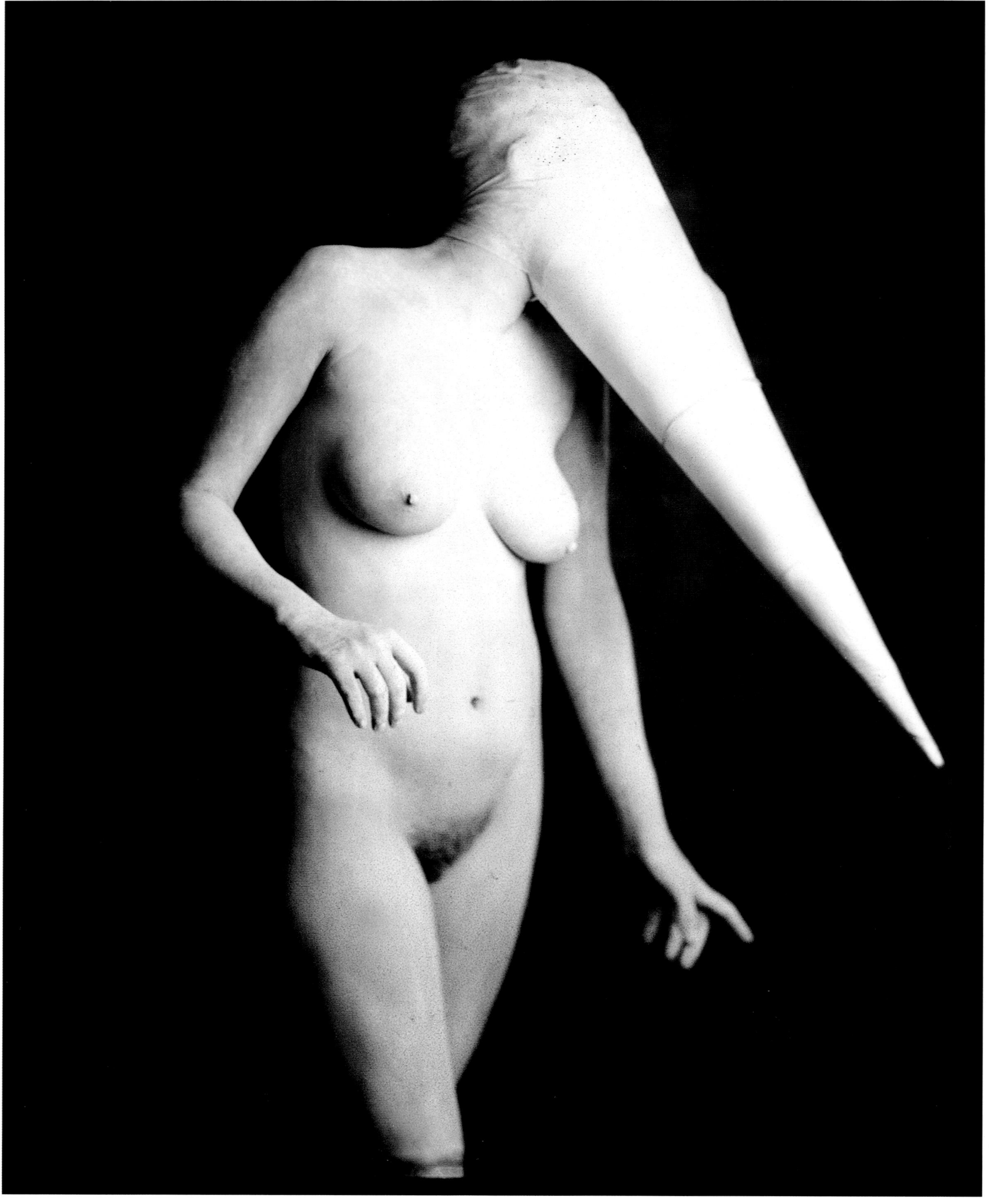

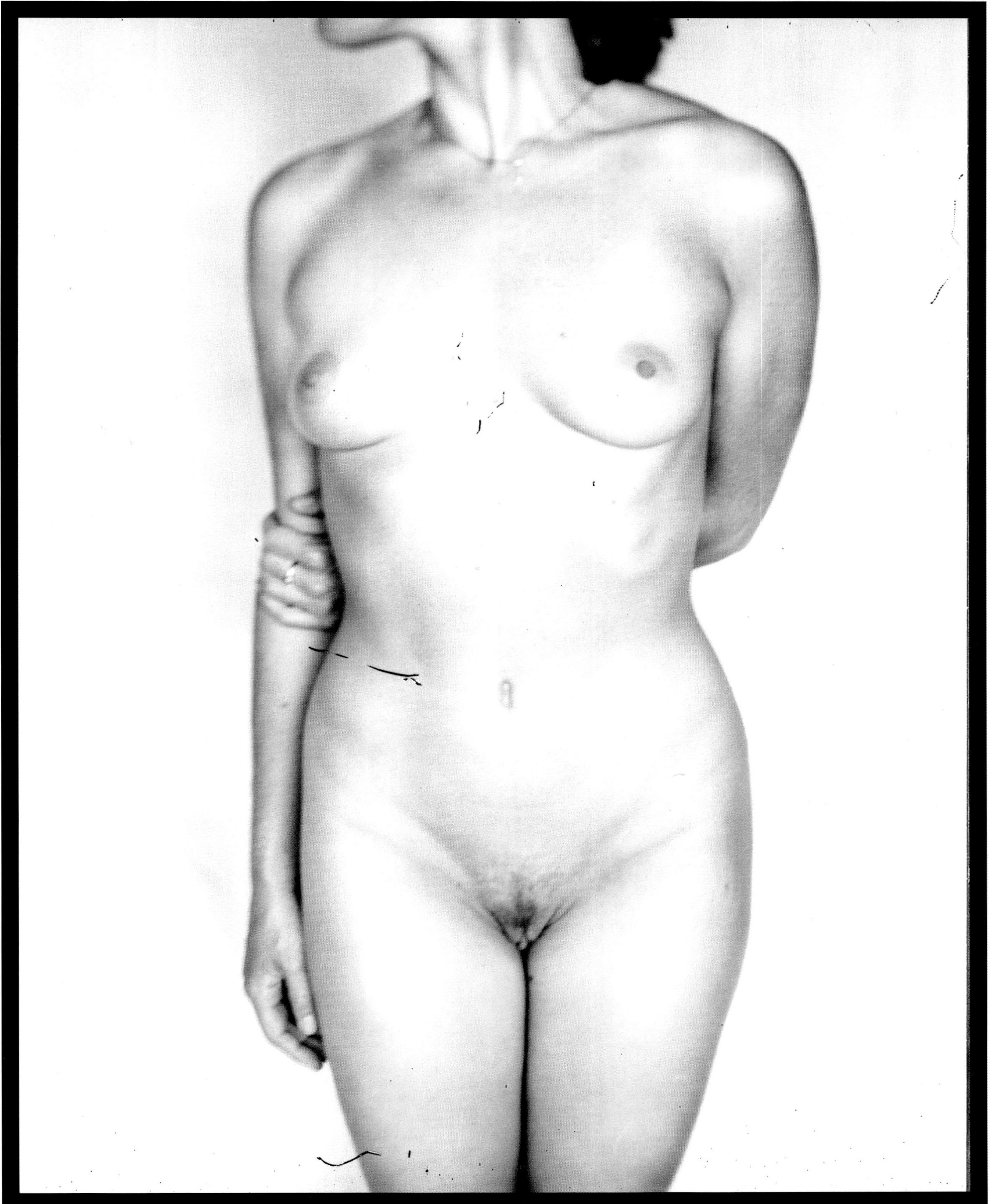

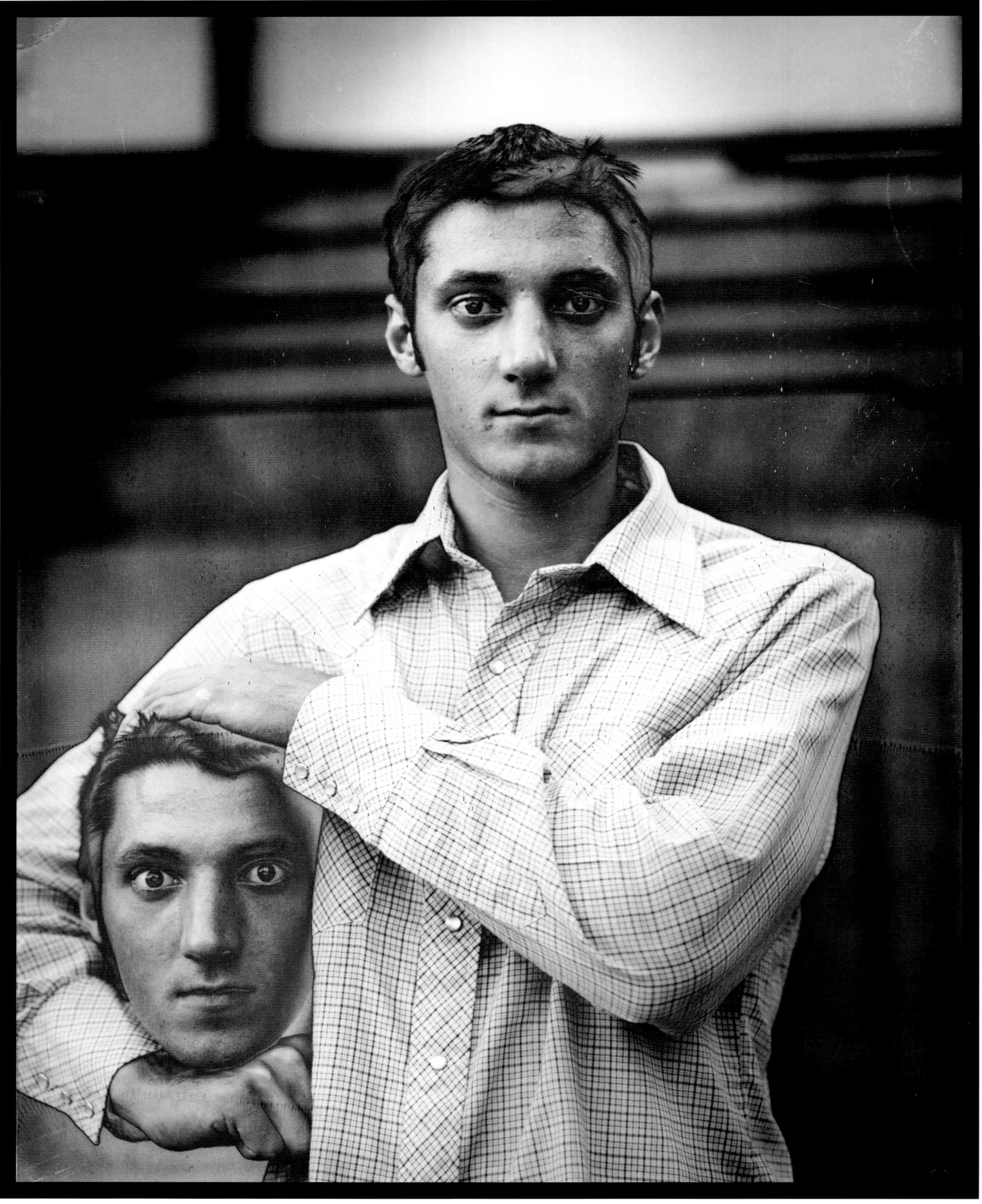

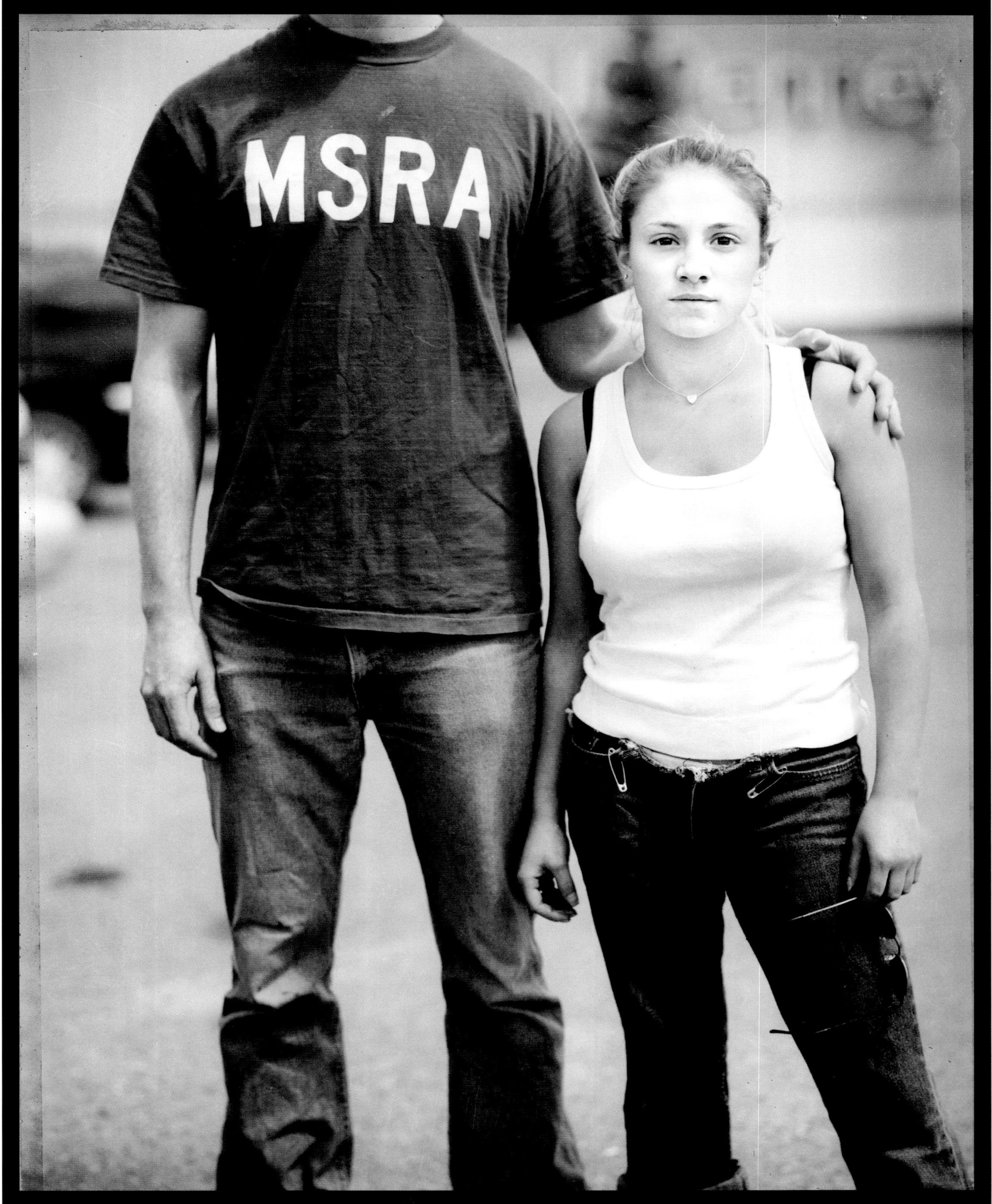
MSRA

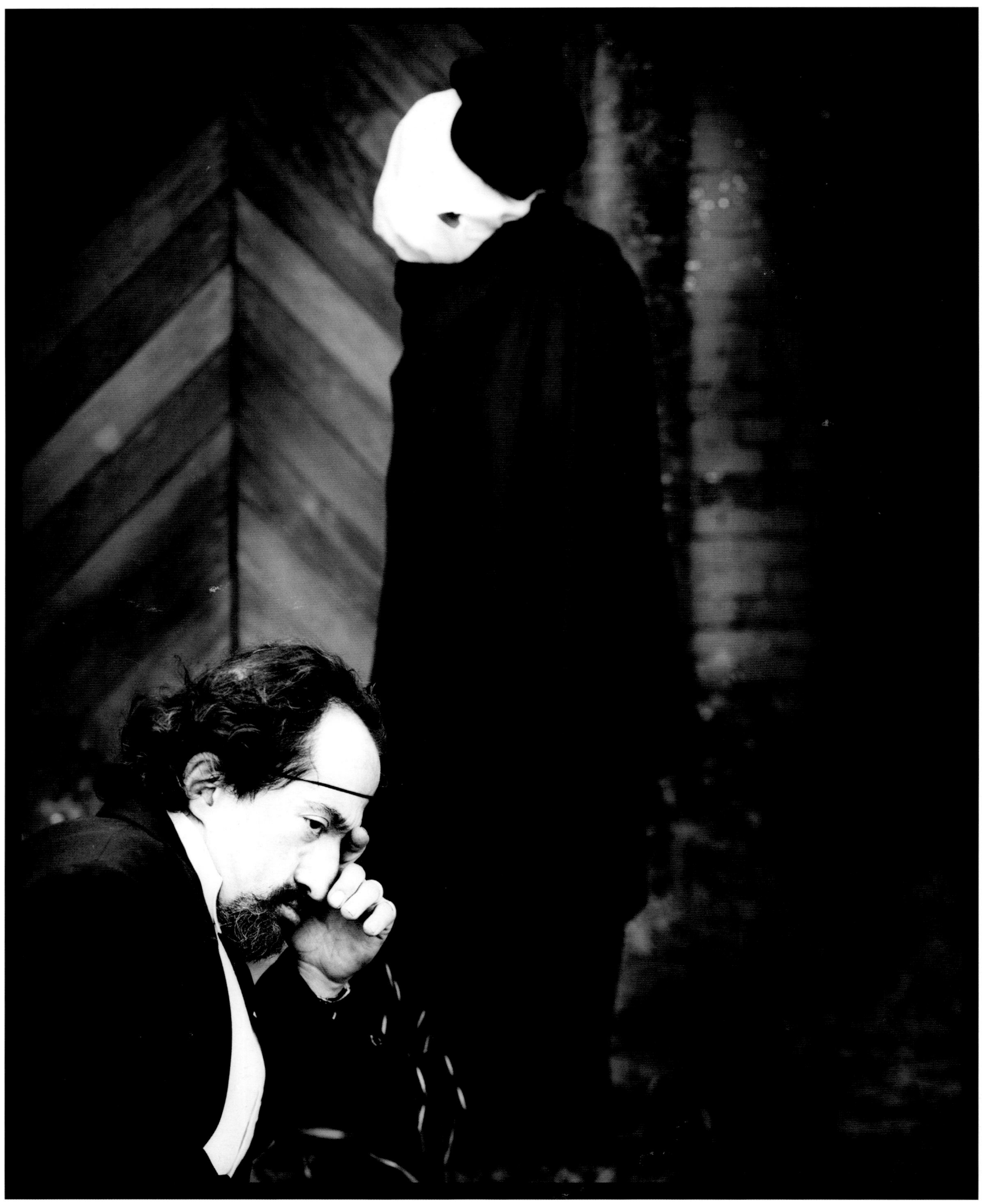

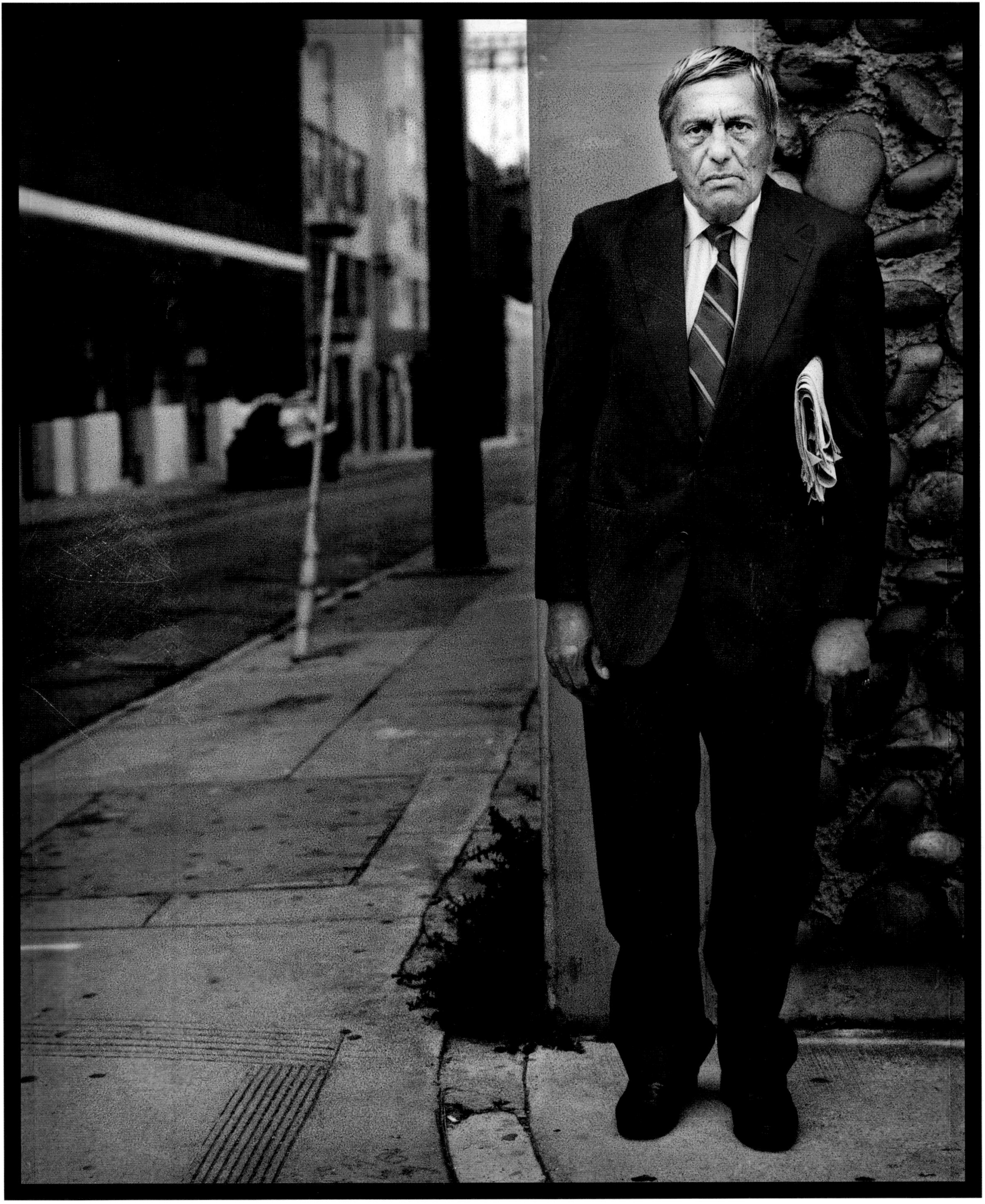

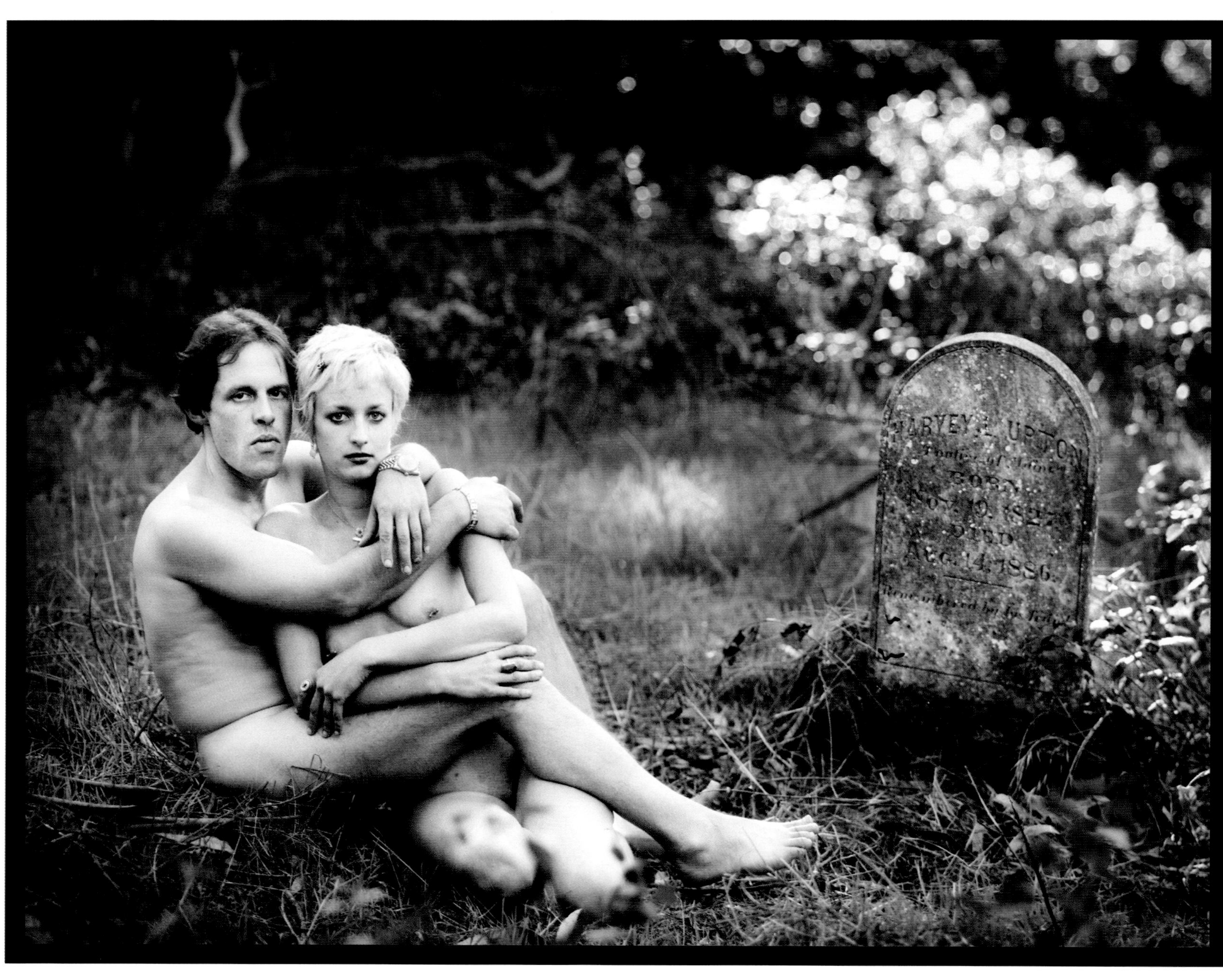
HARVEY L. UPTON
BORN
DIED
AUG. 14, 1886

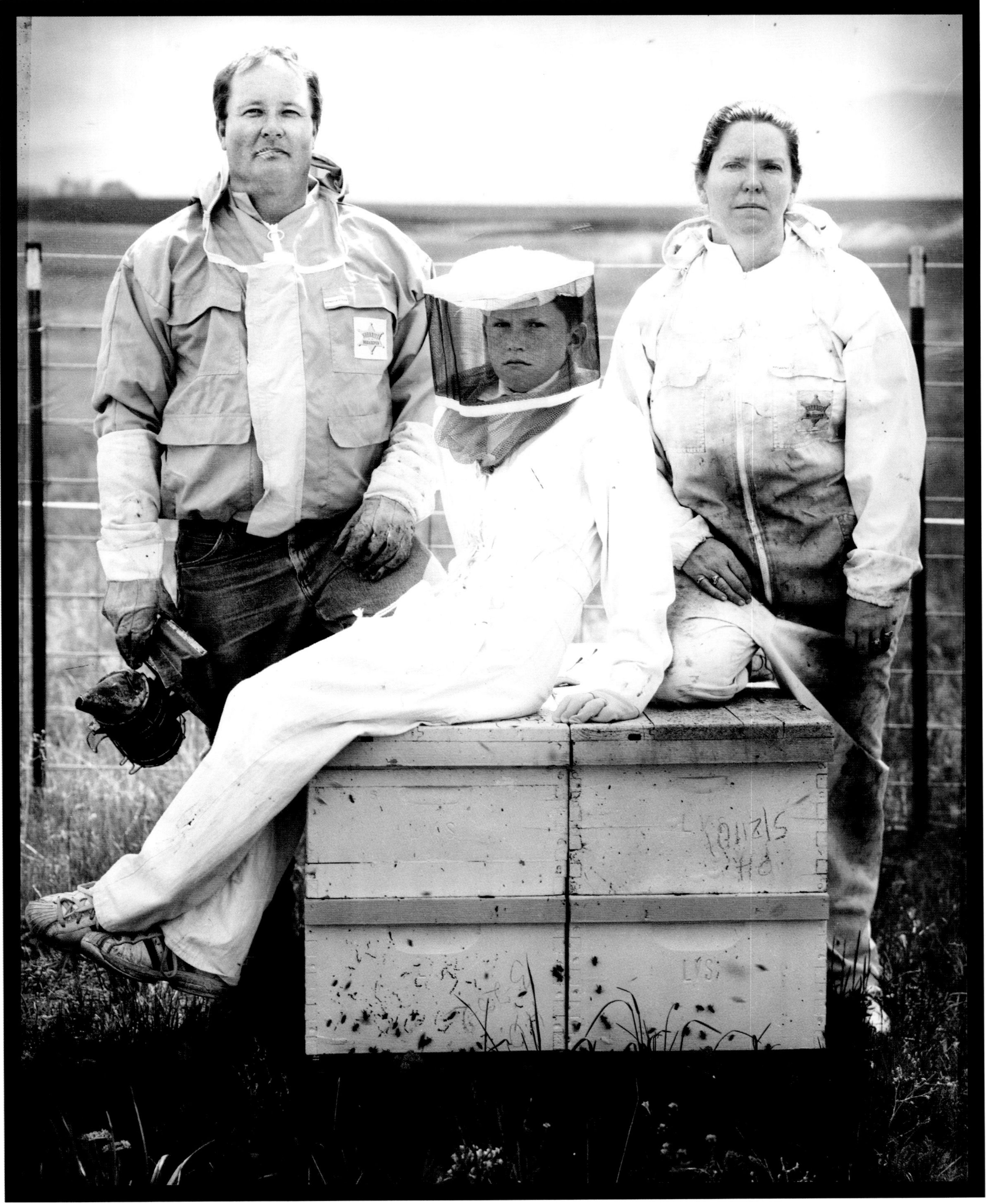

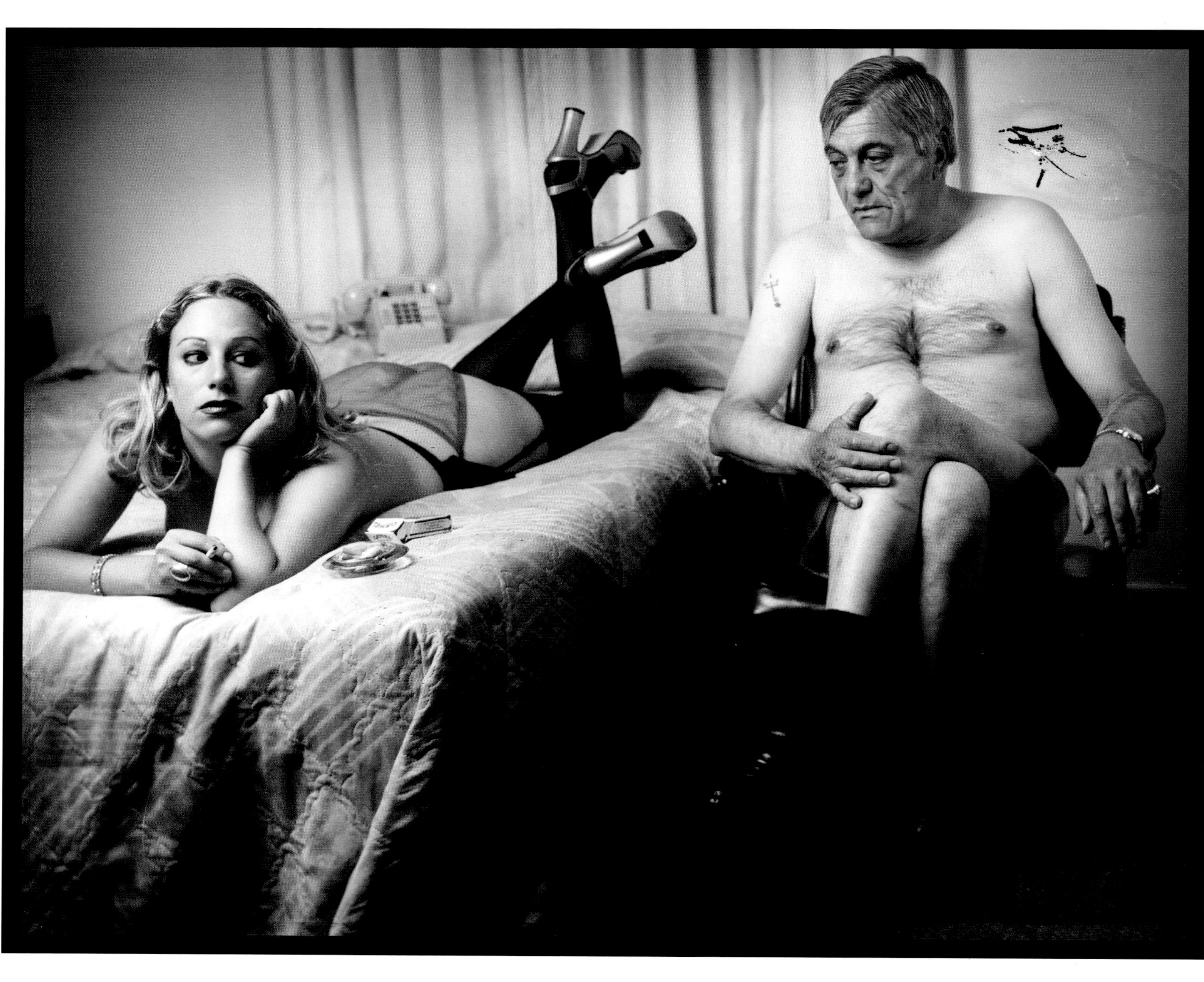

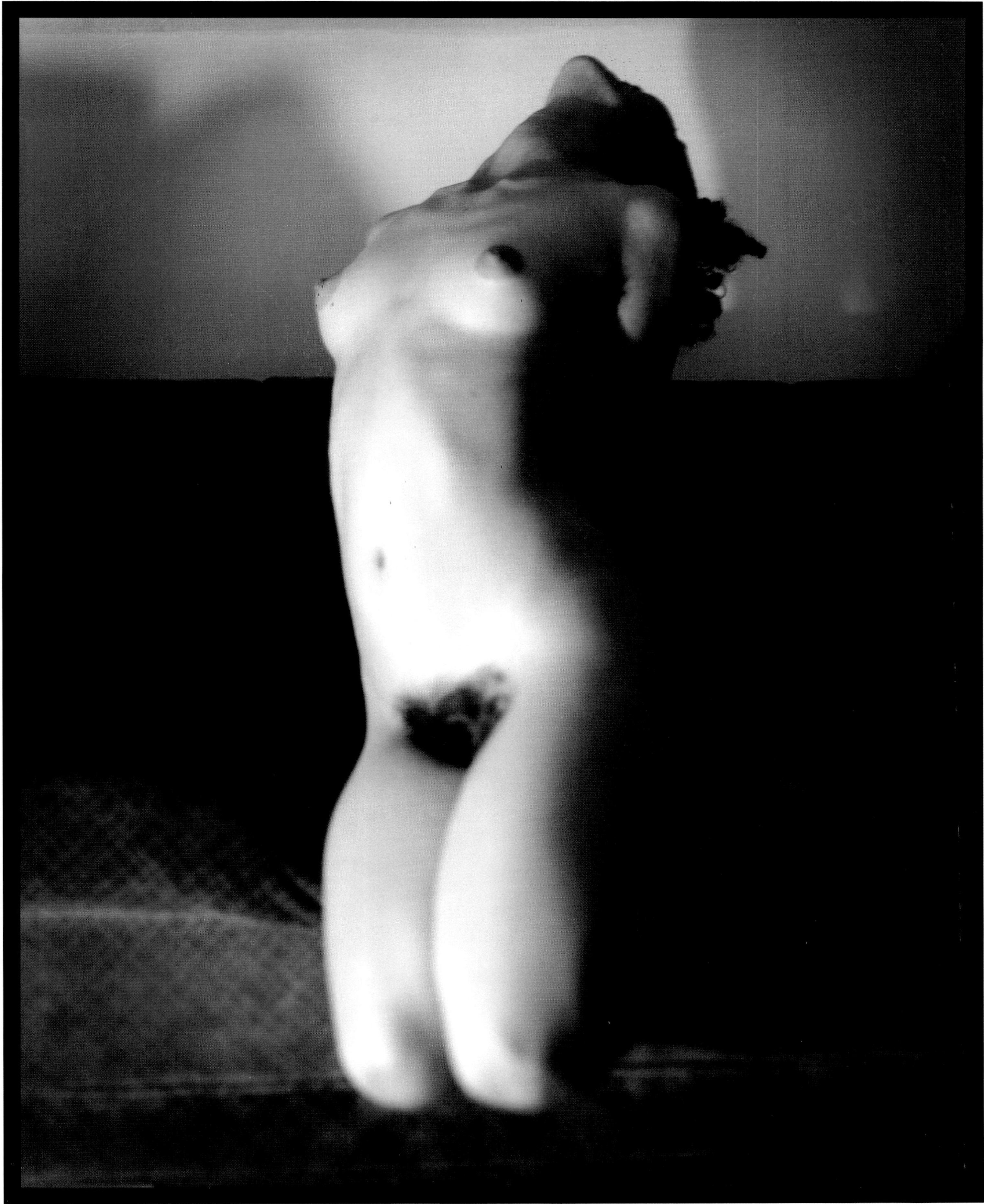

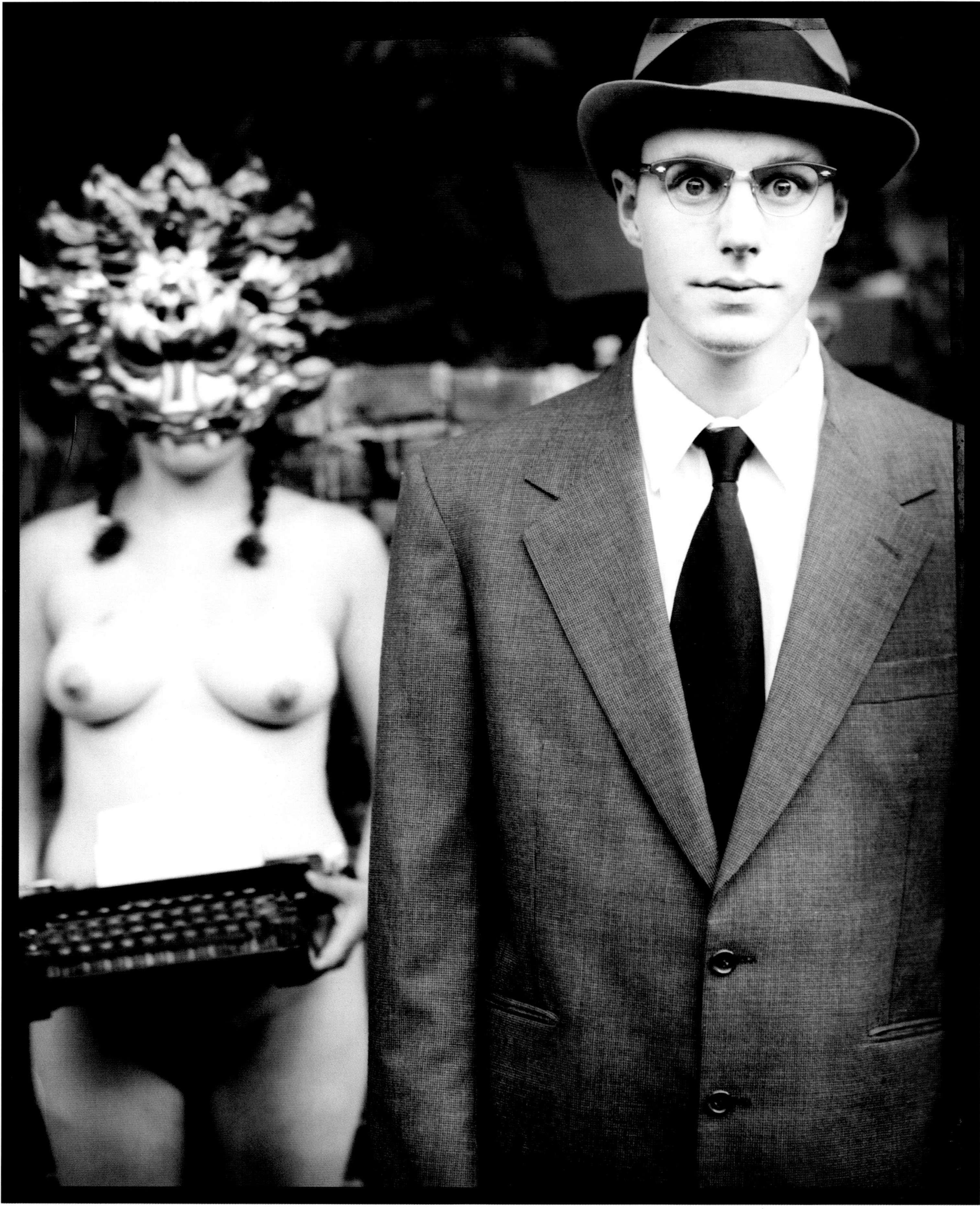

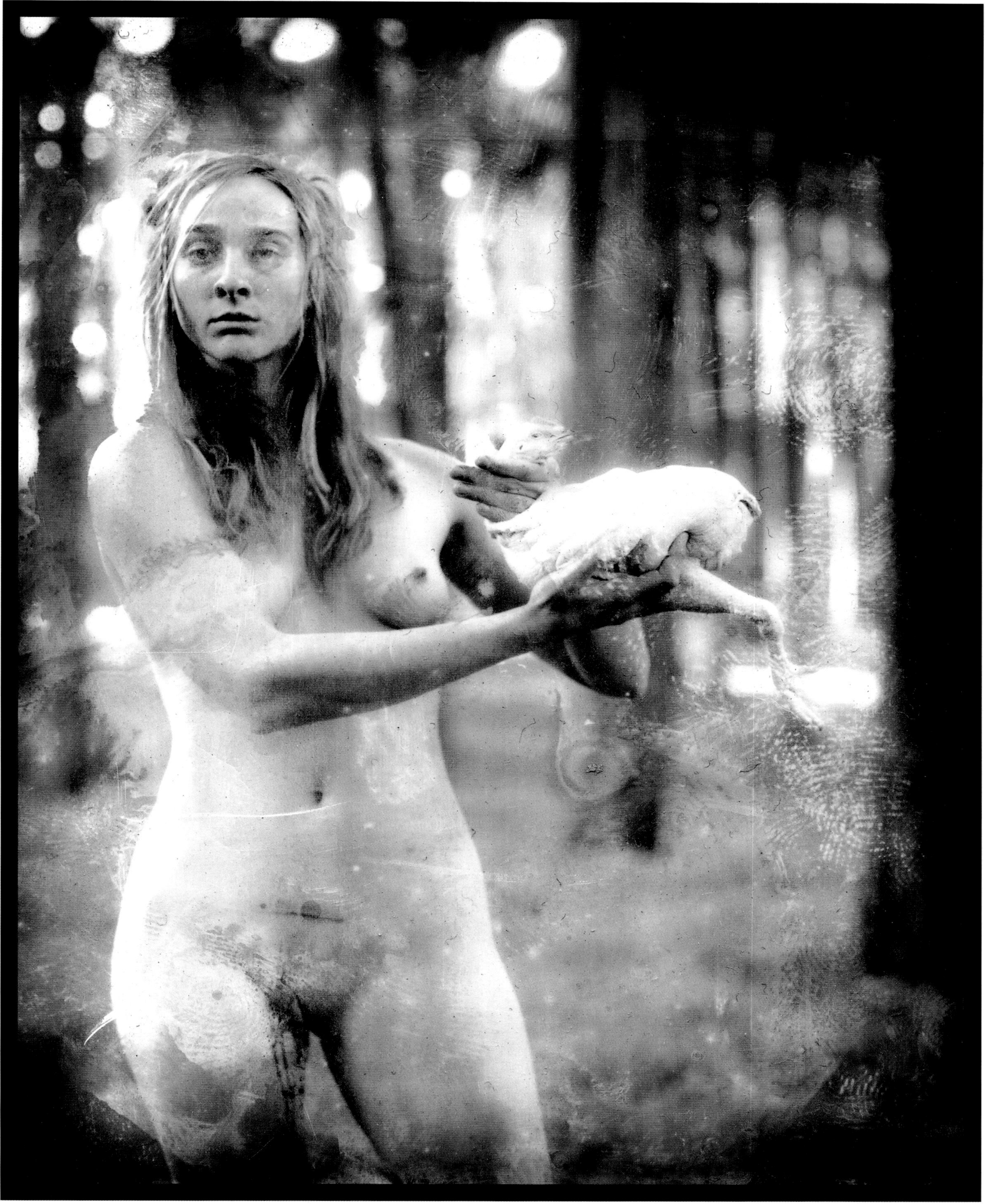

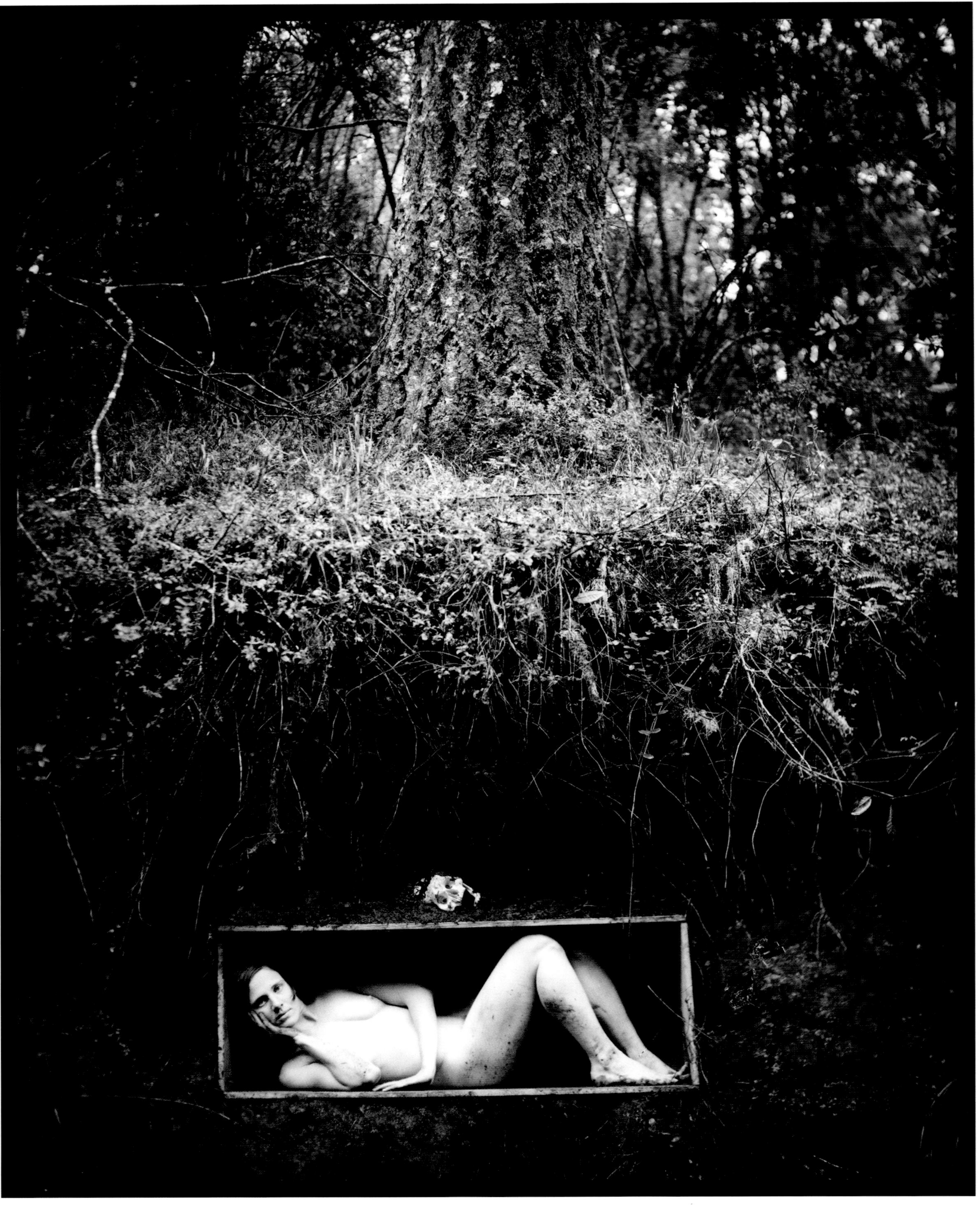

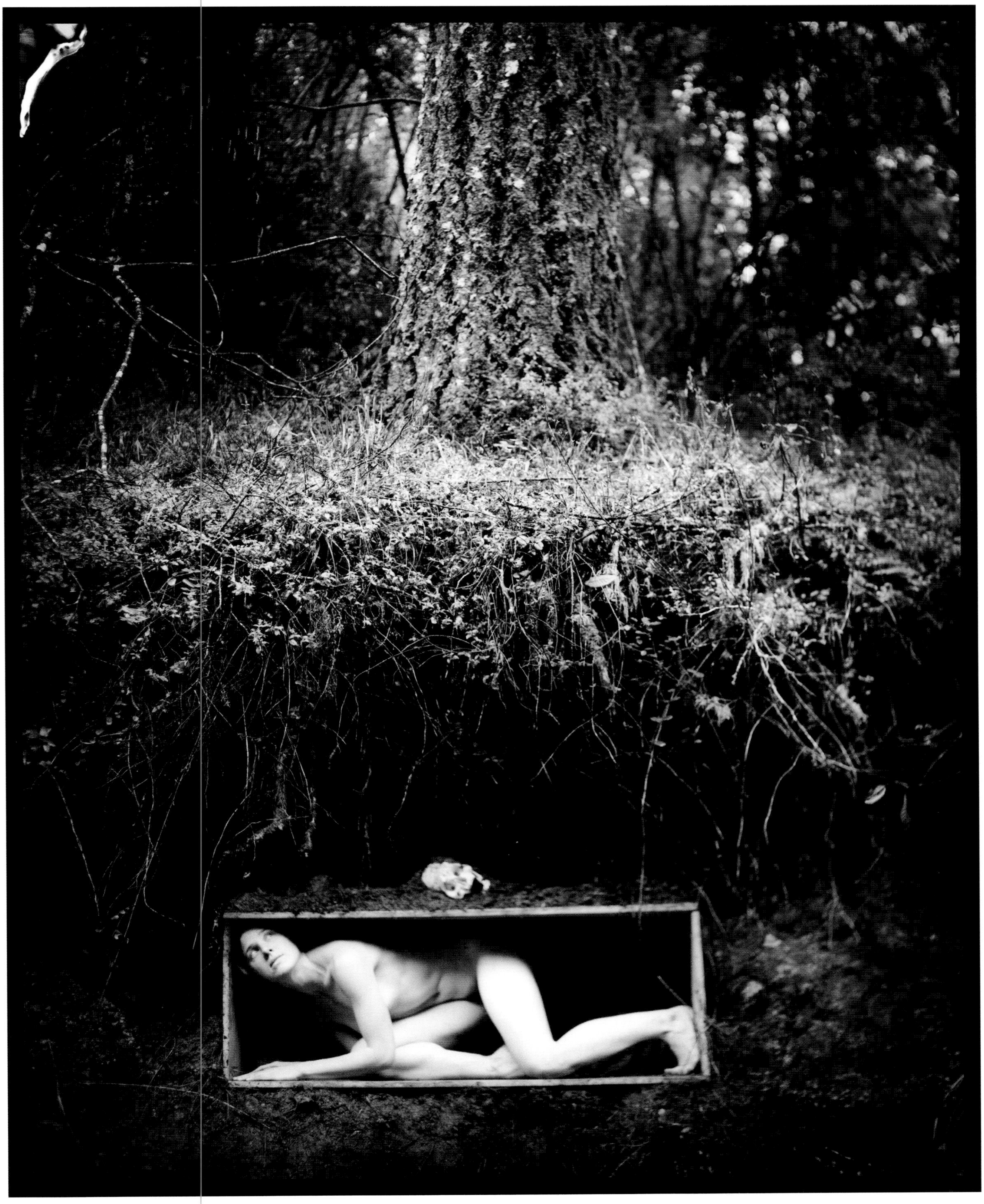

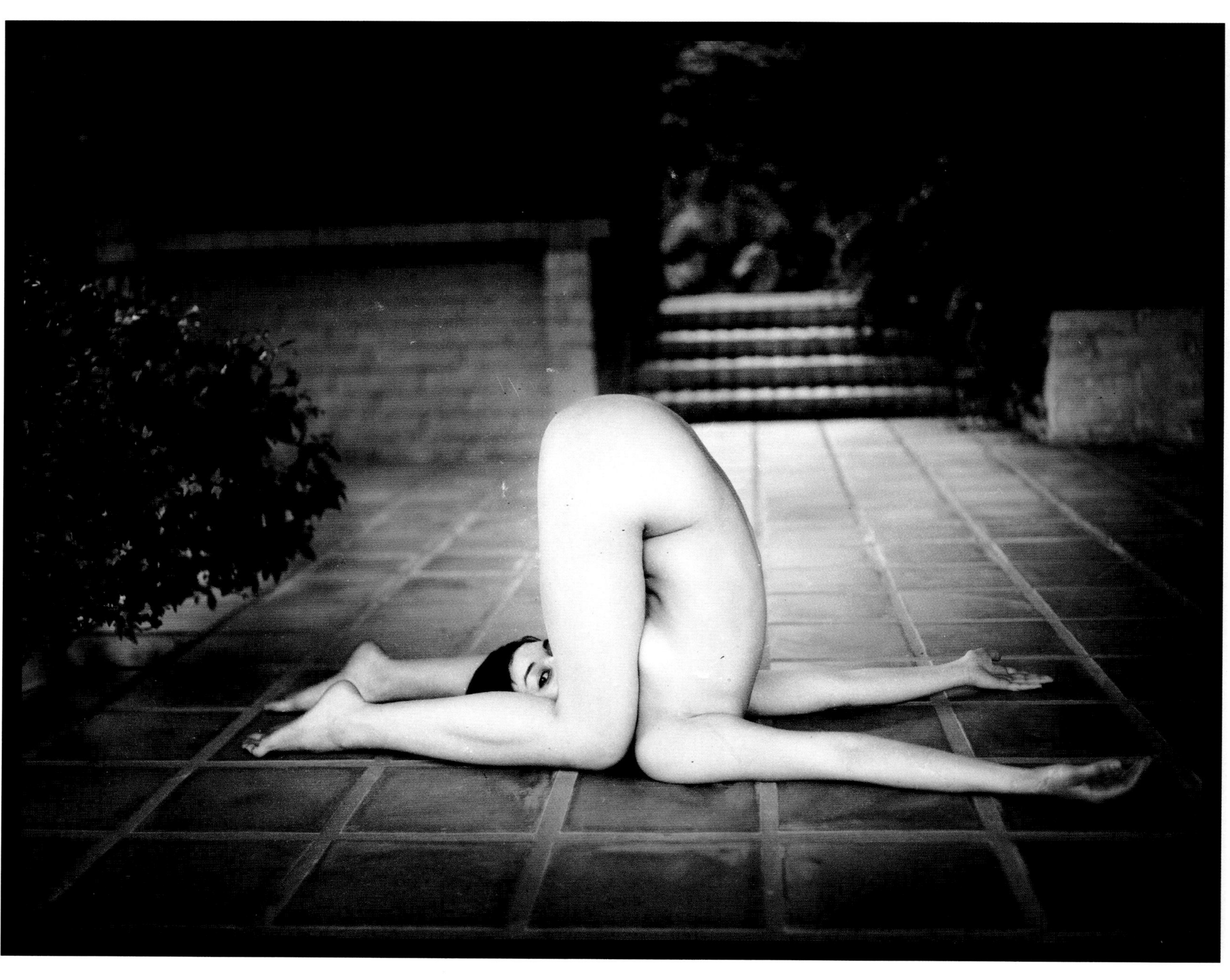

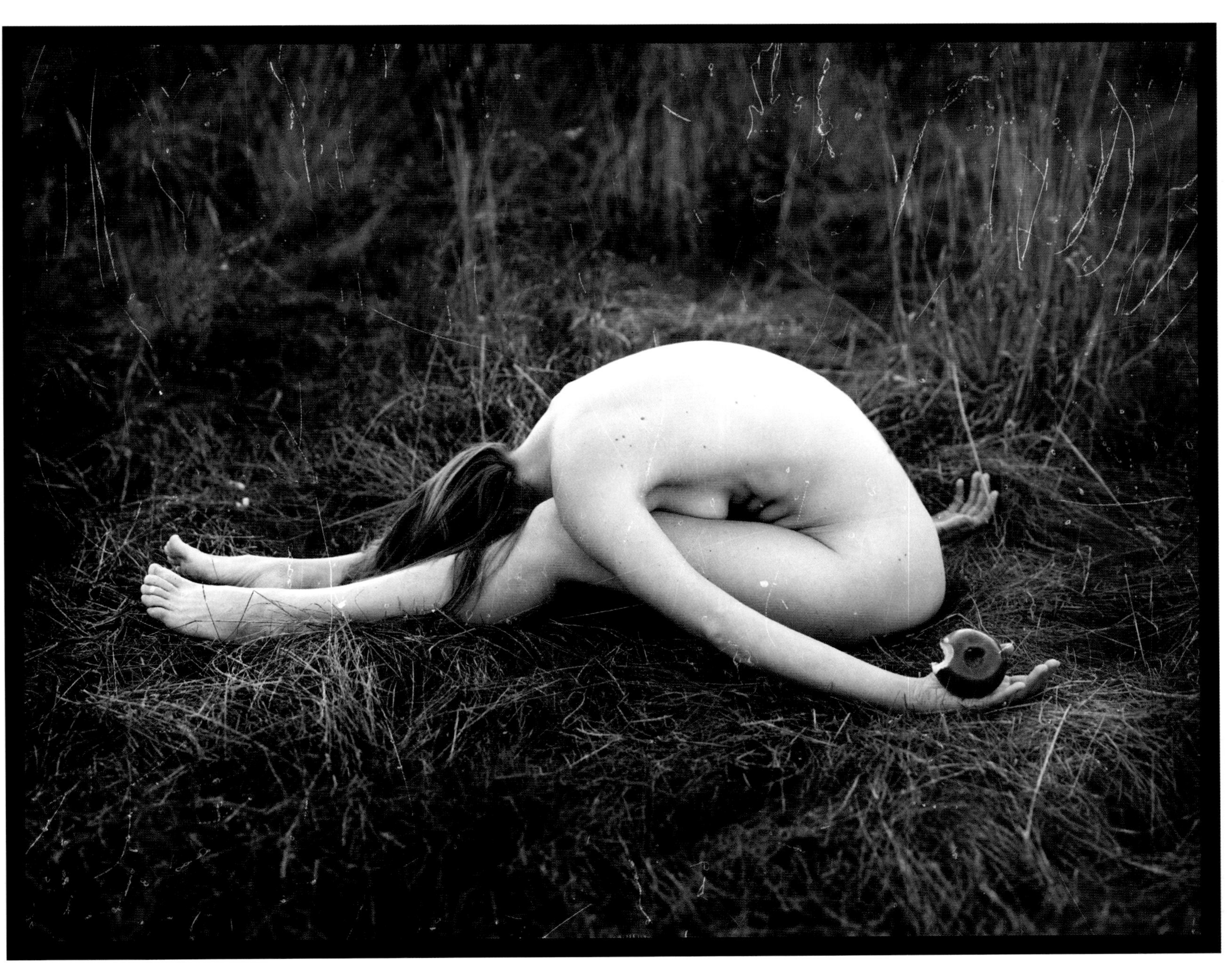

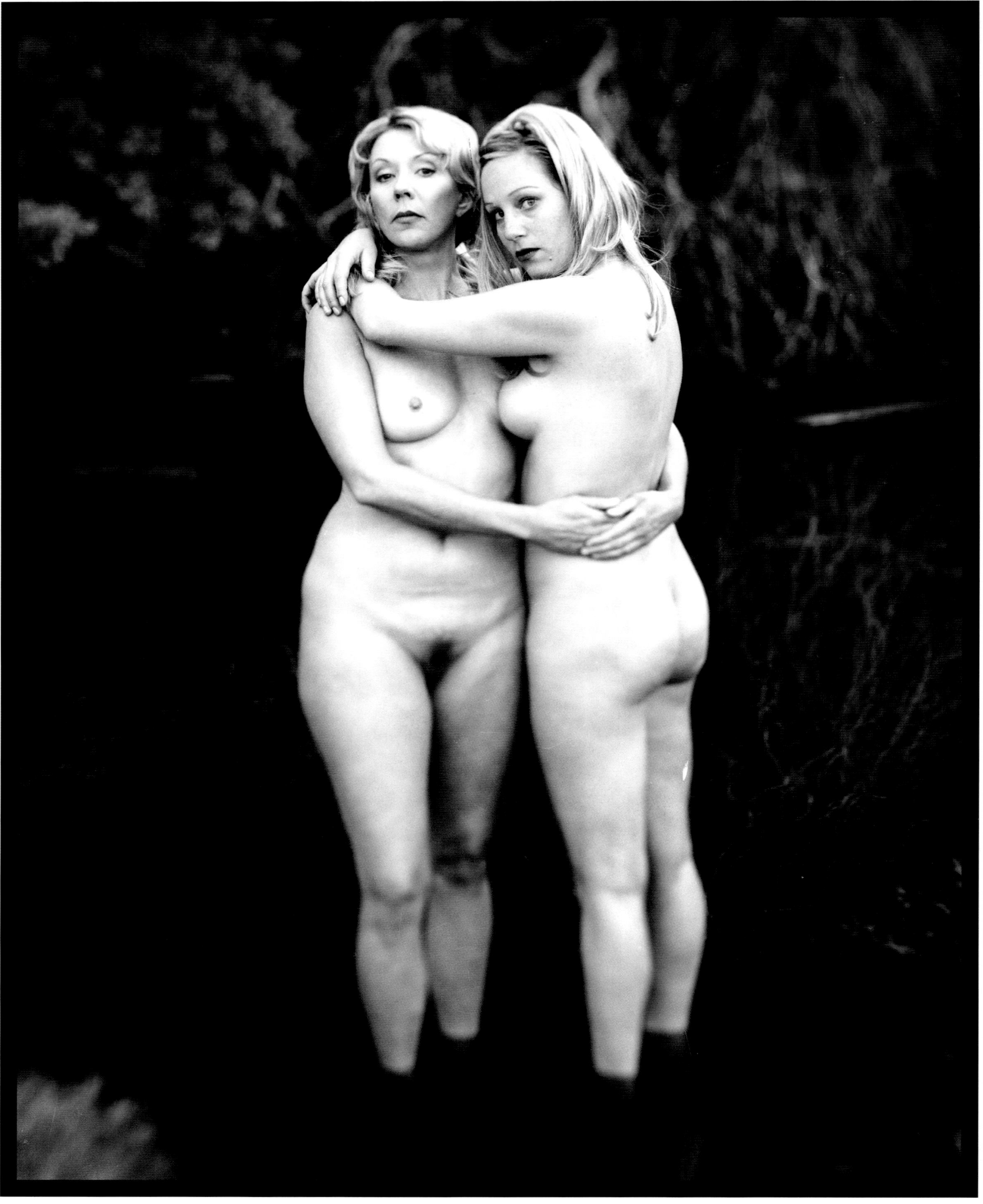

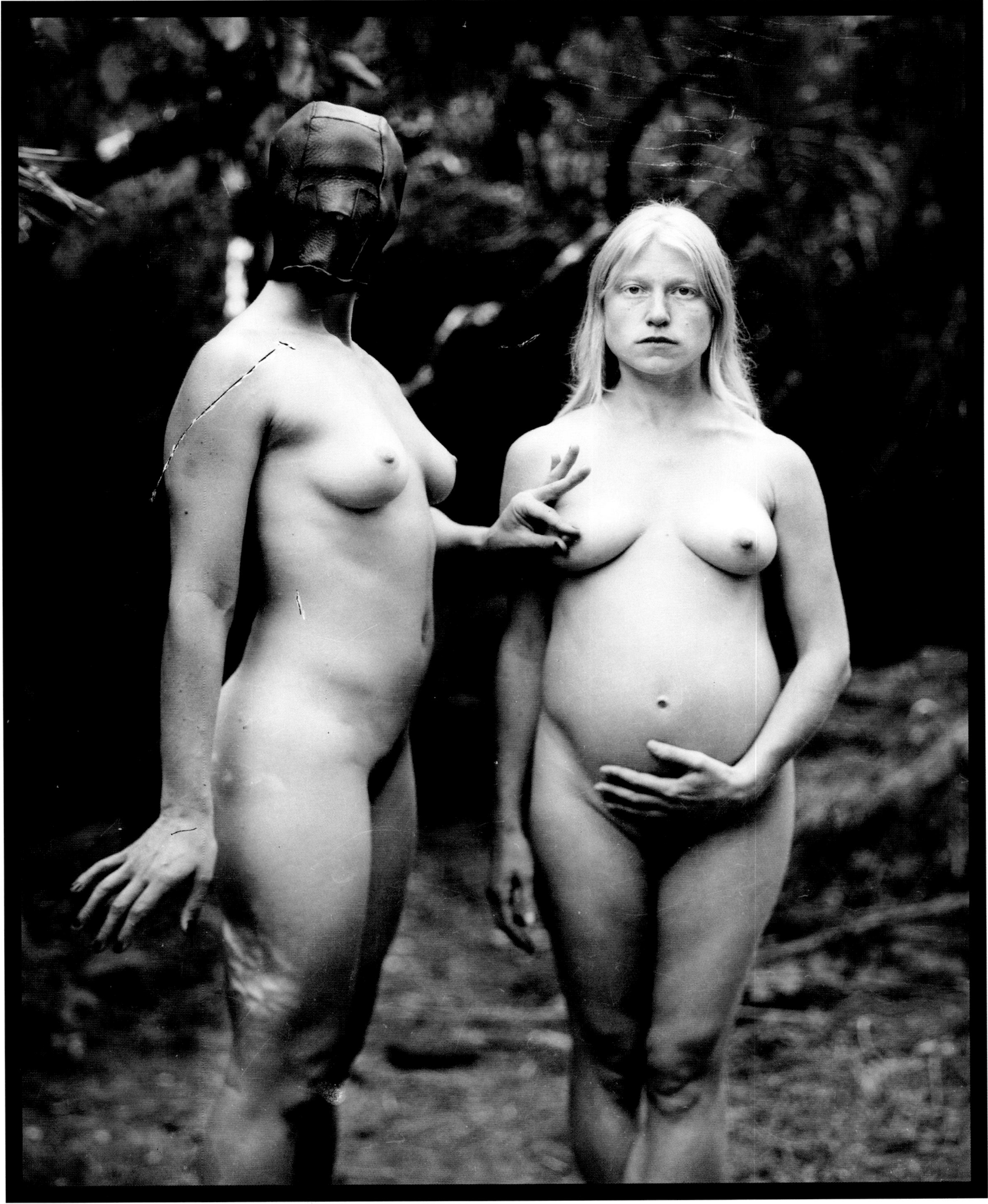

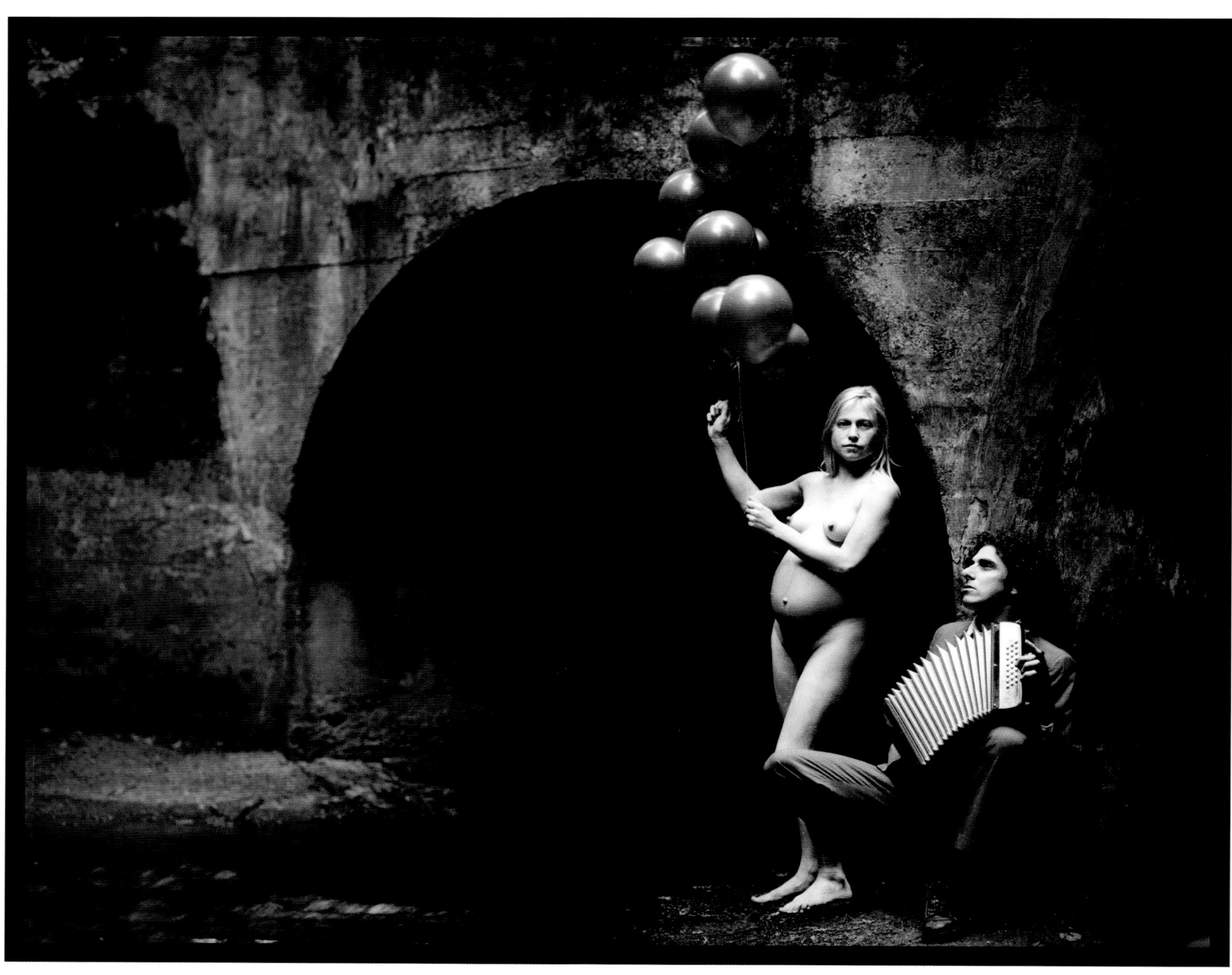

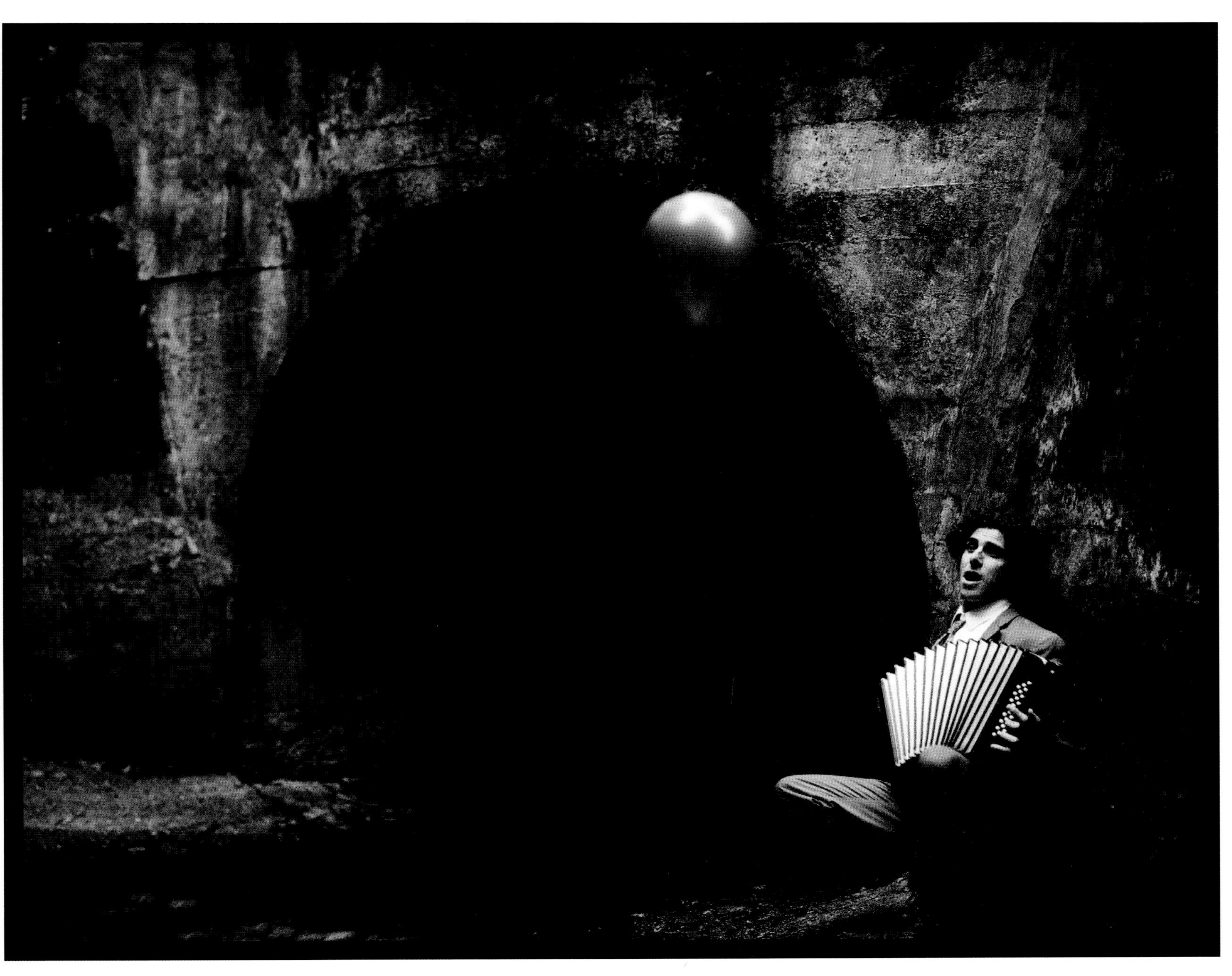

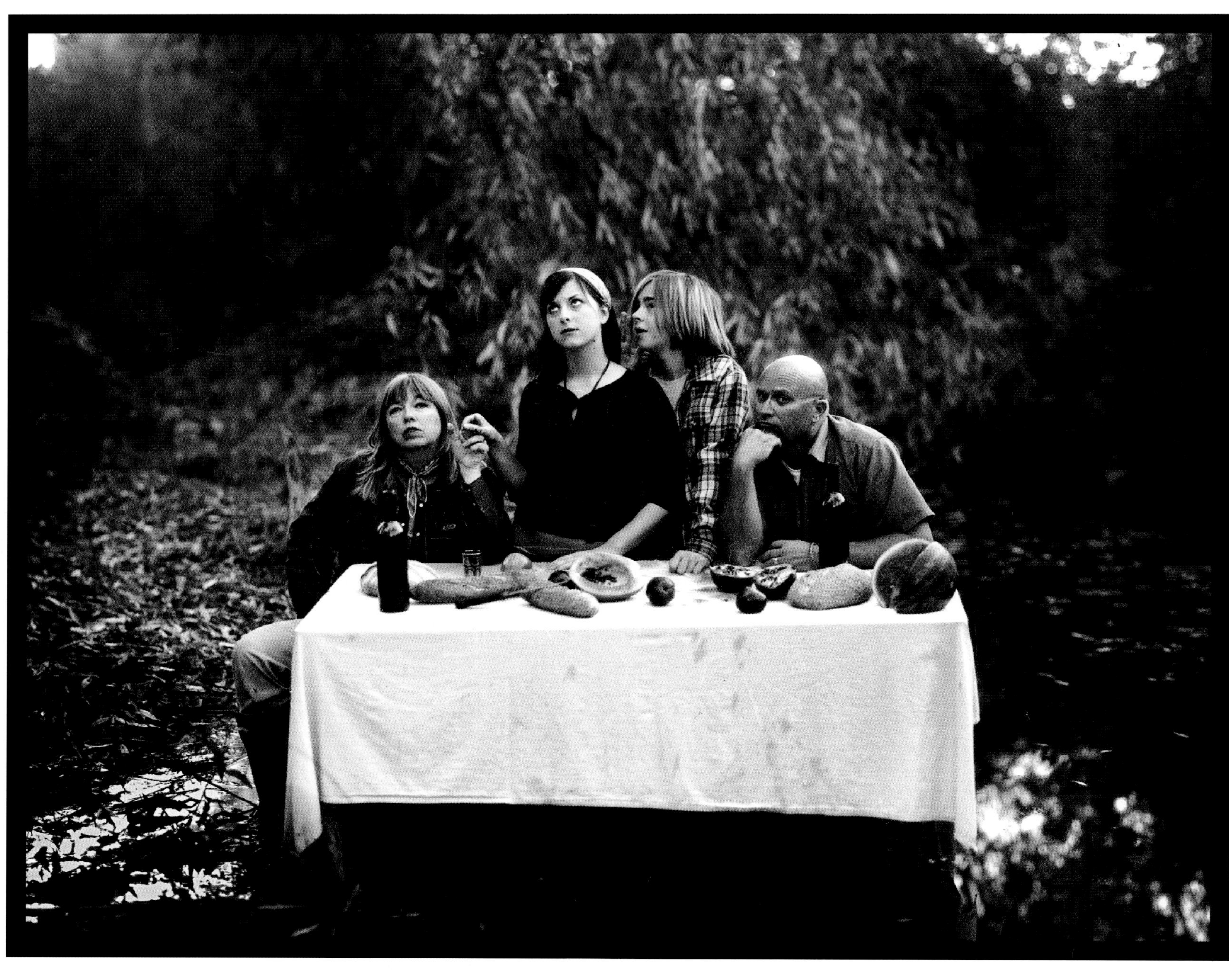

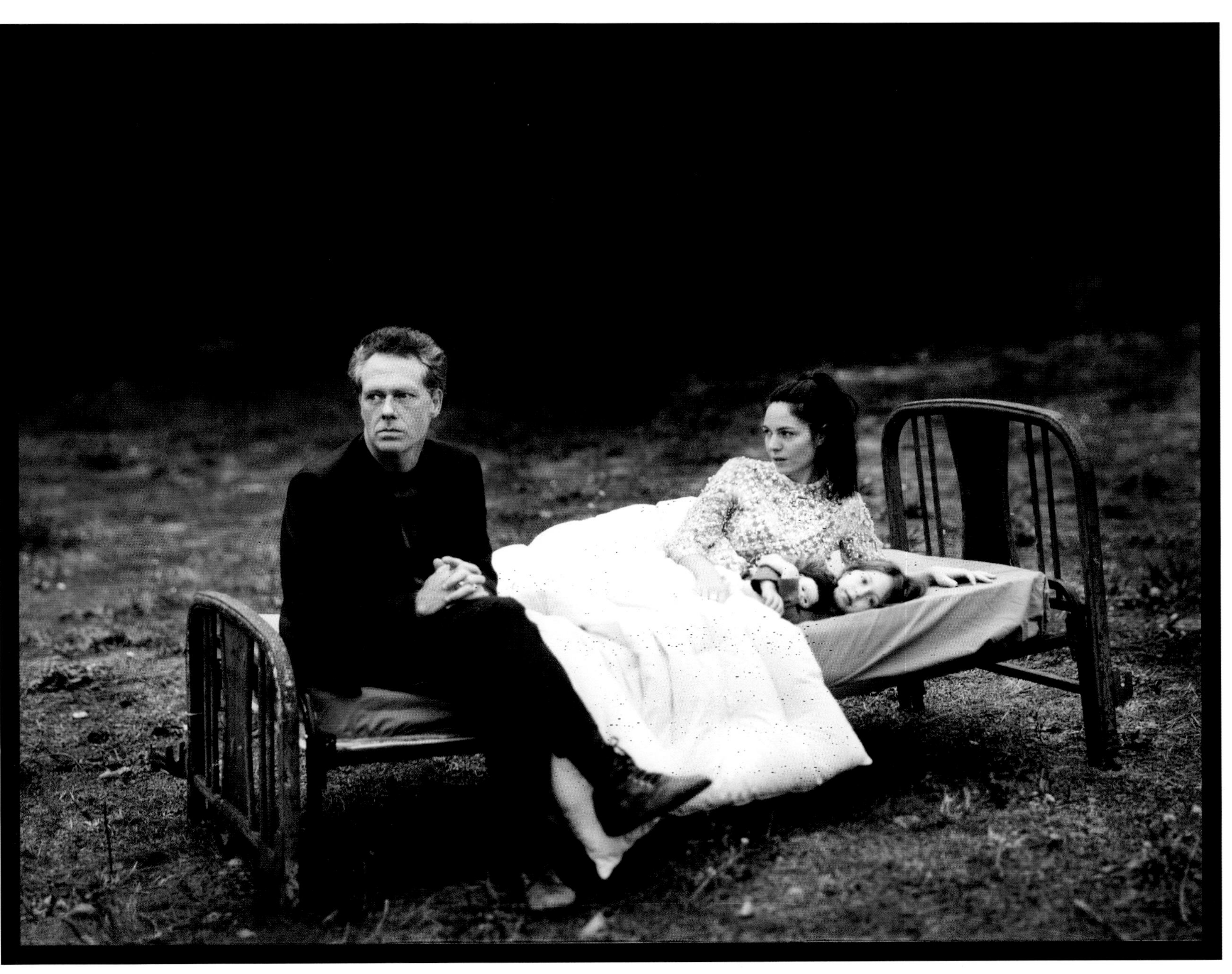

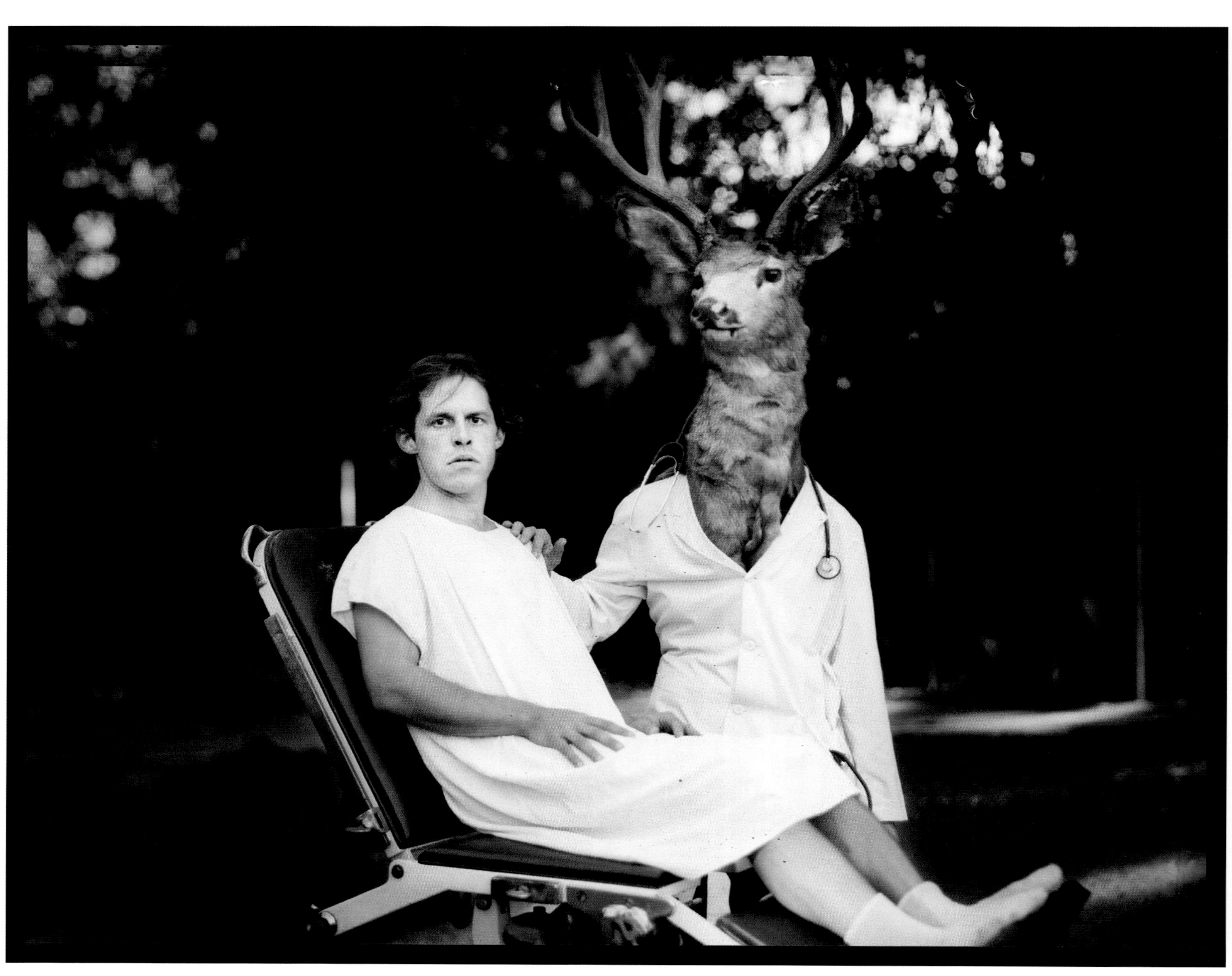

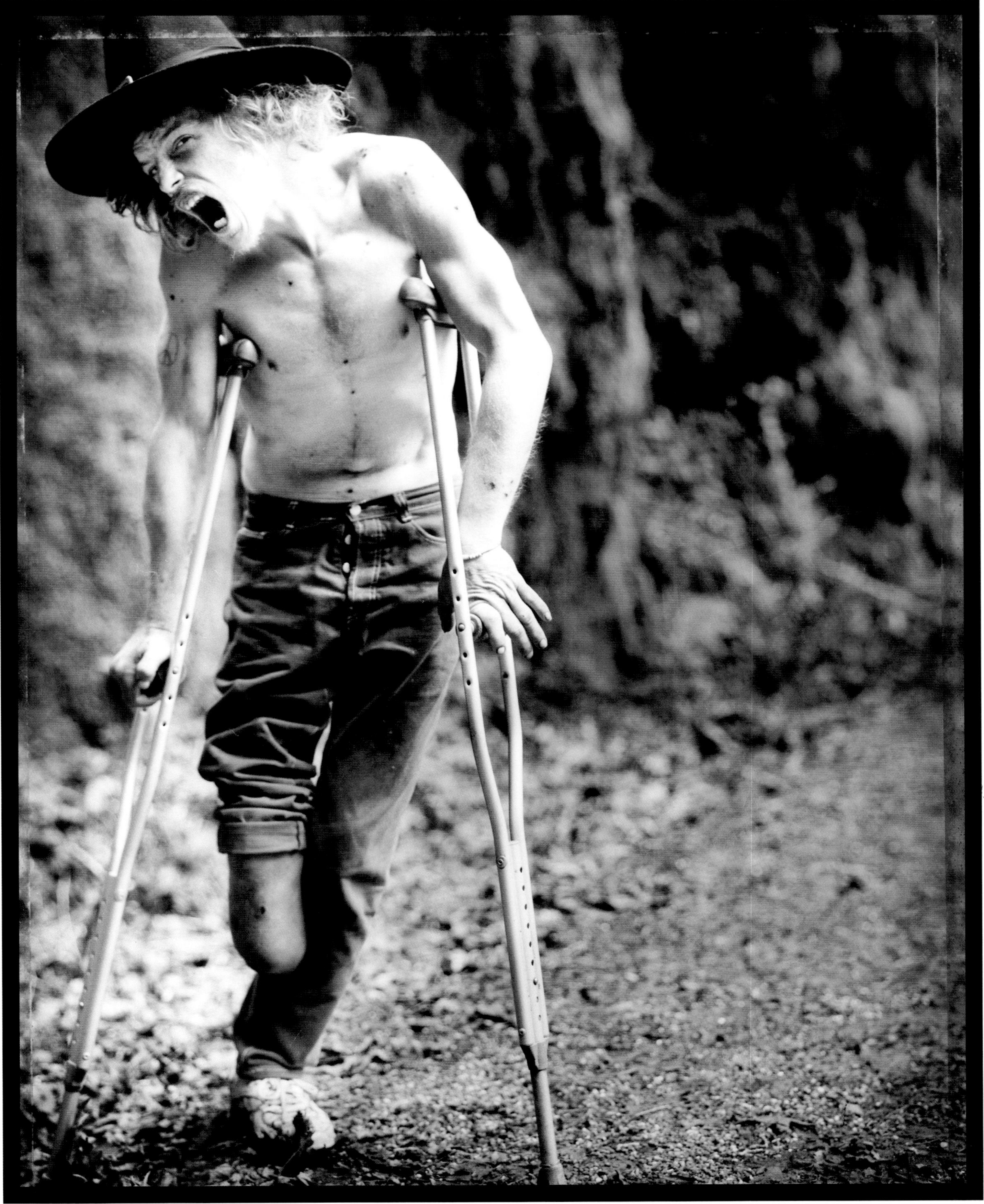

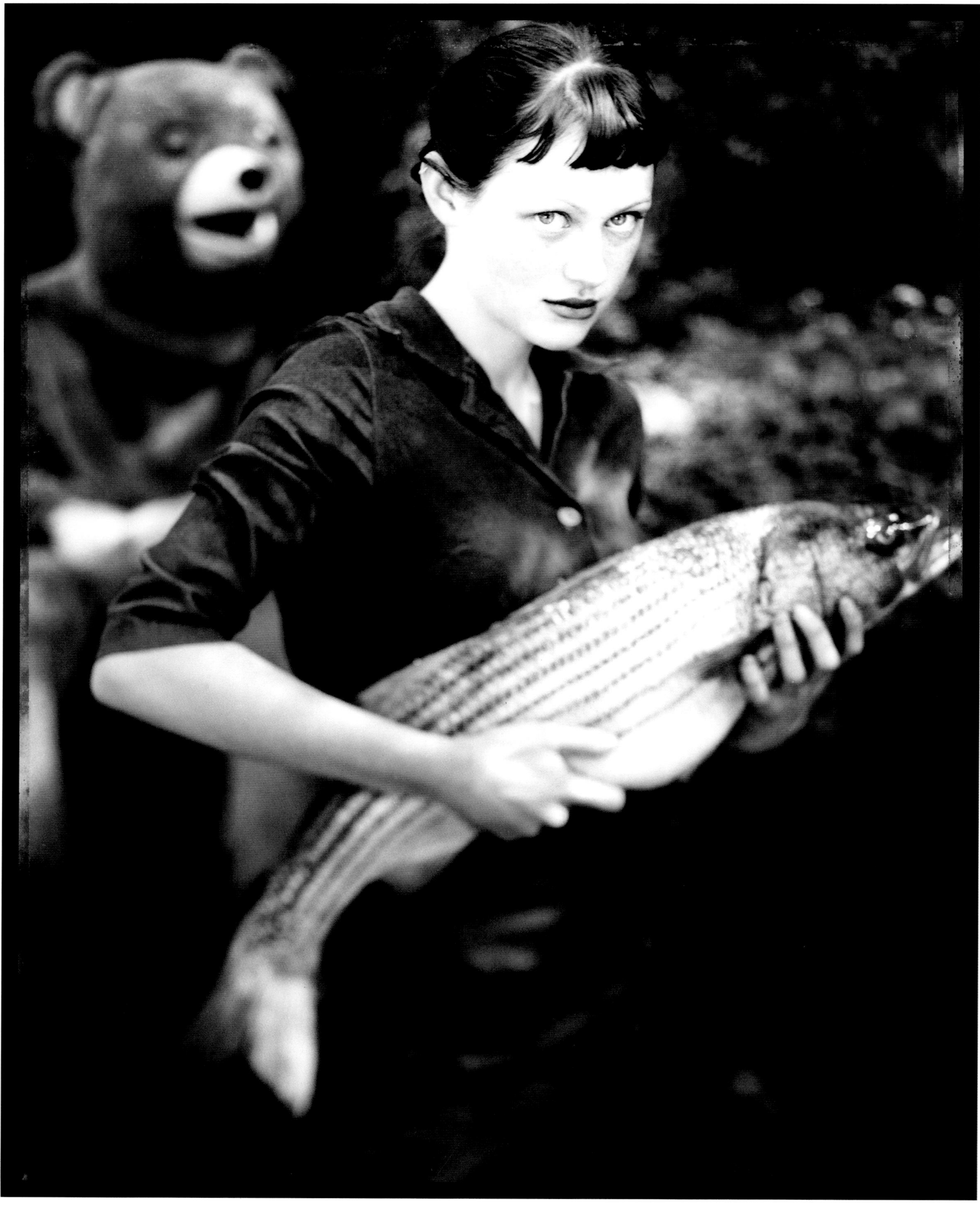

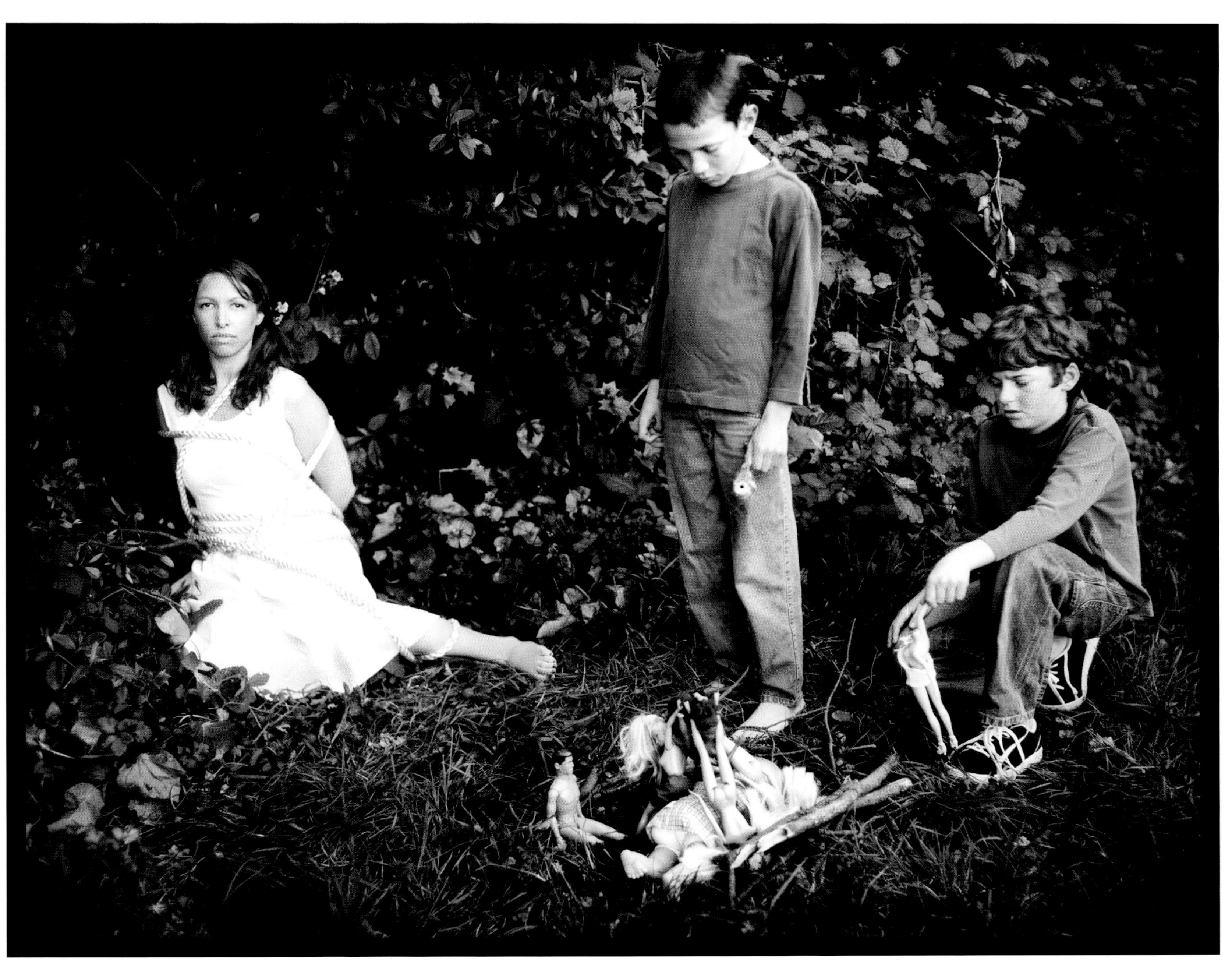

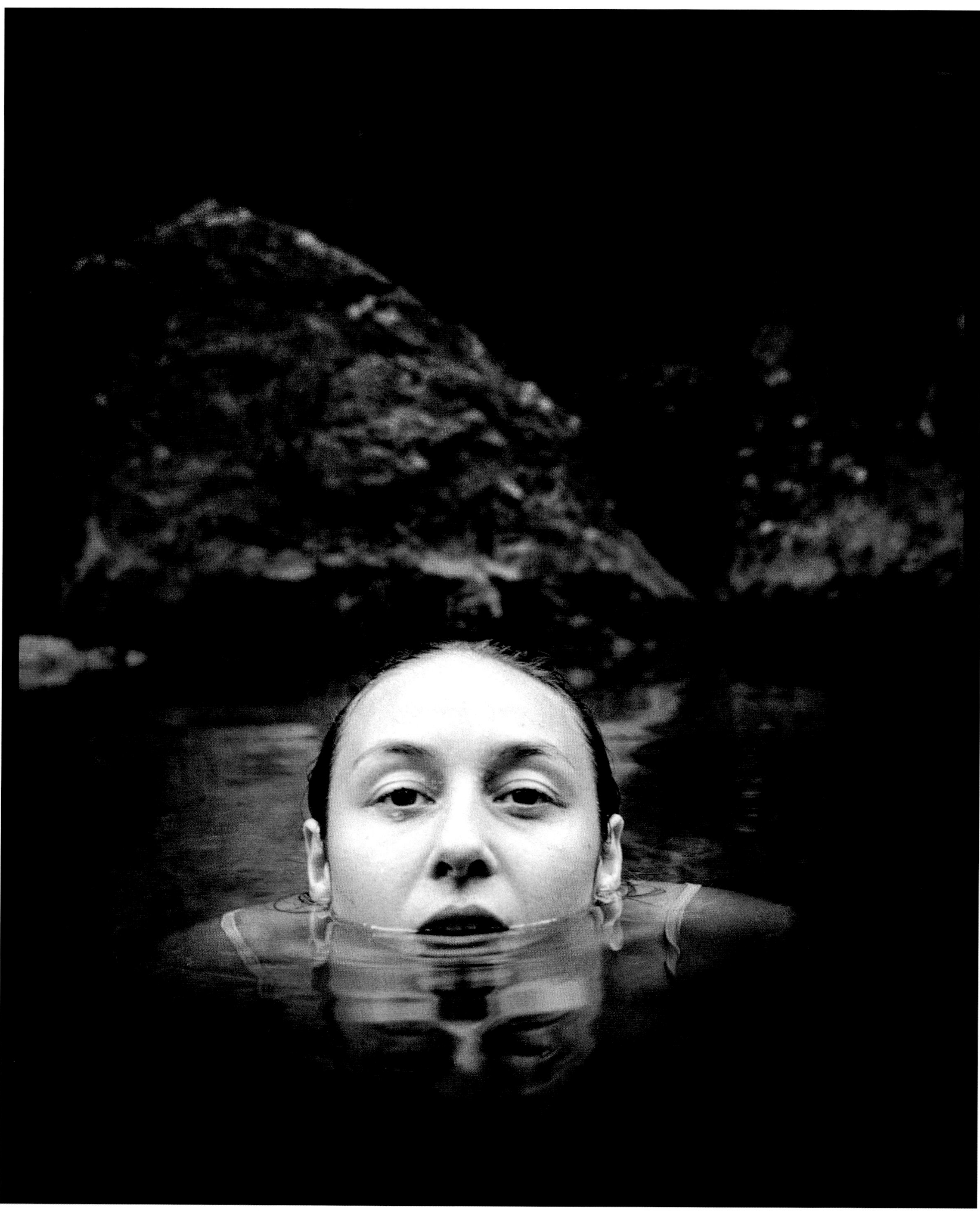

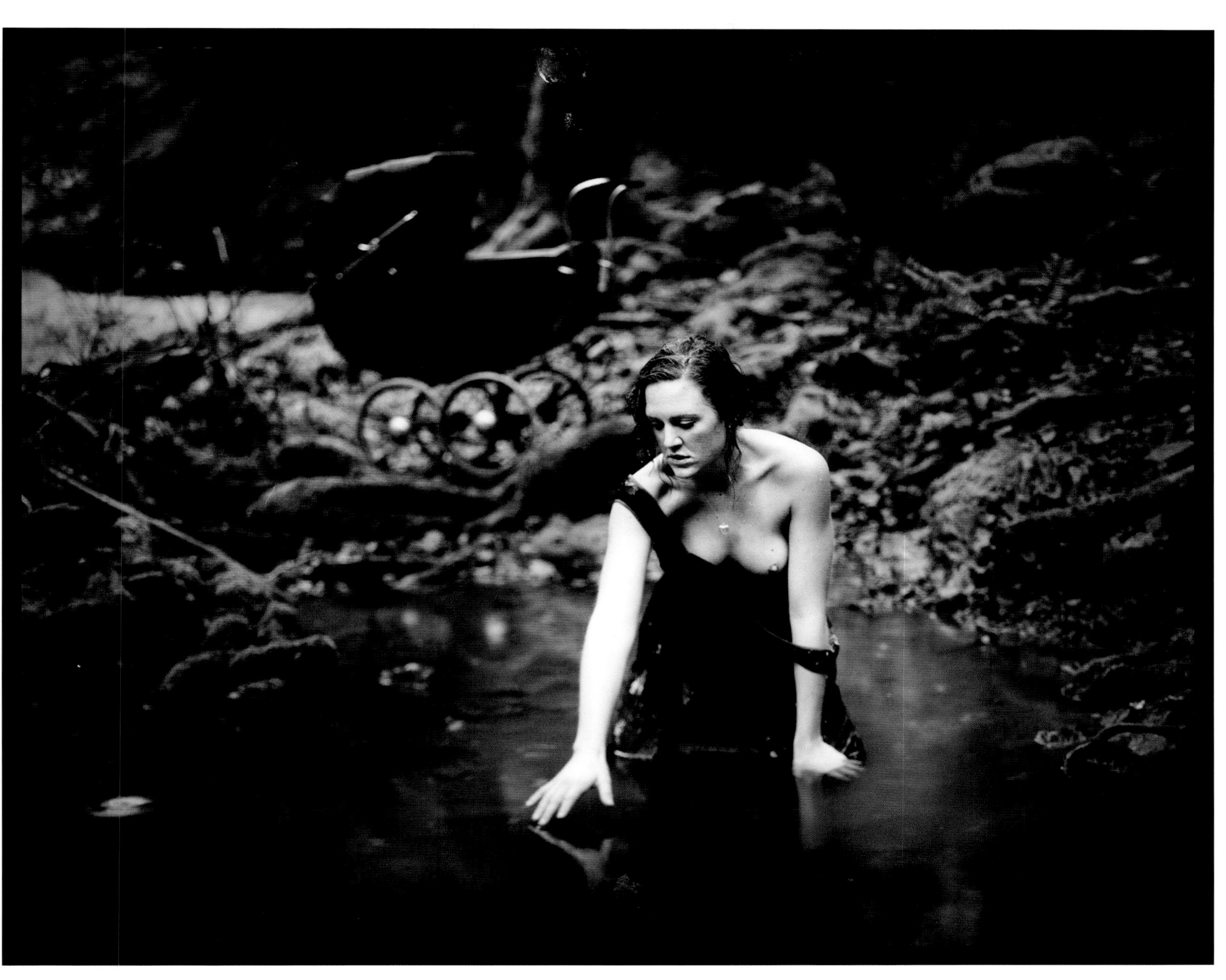

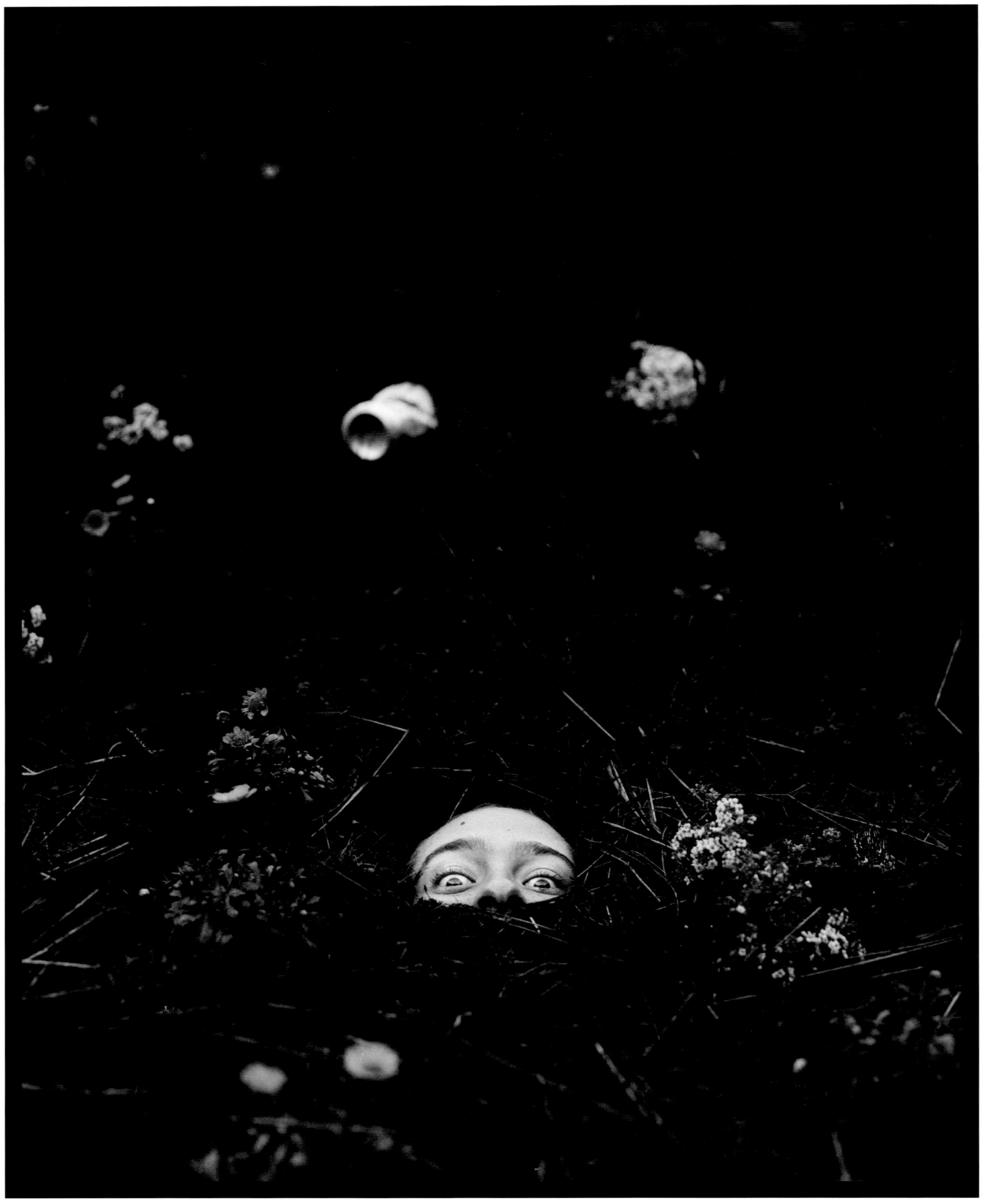

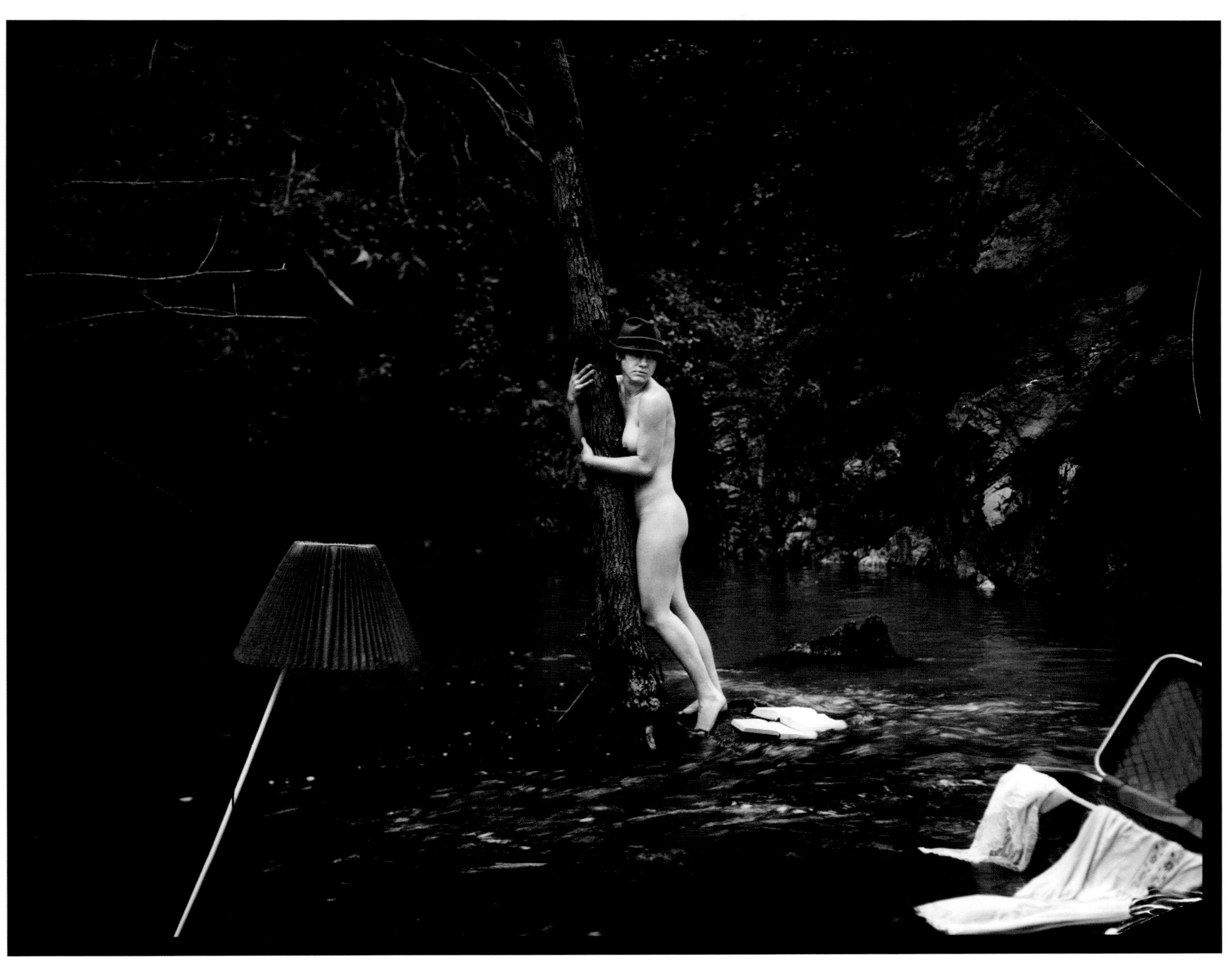

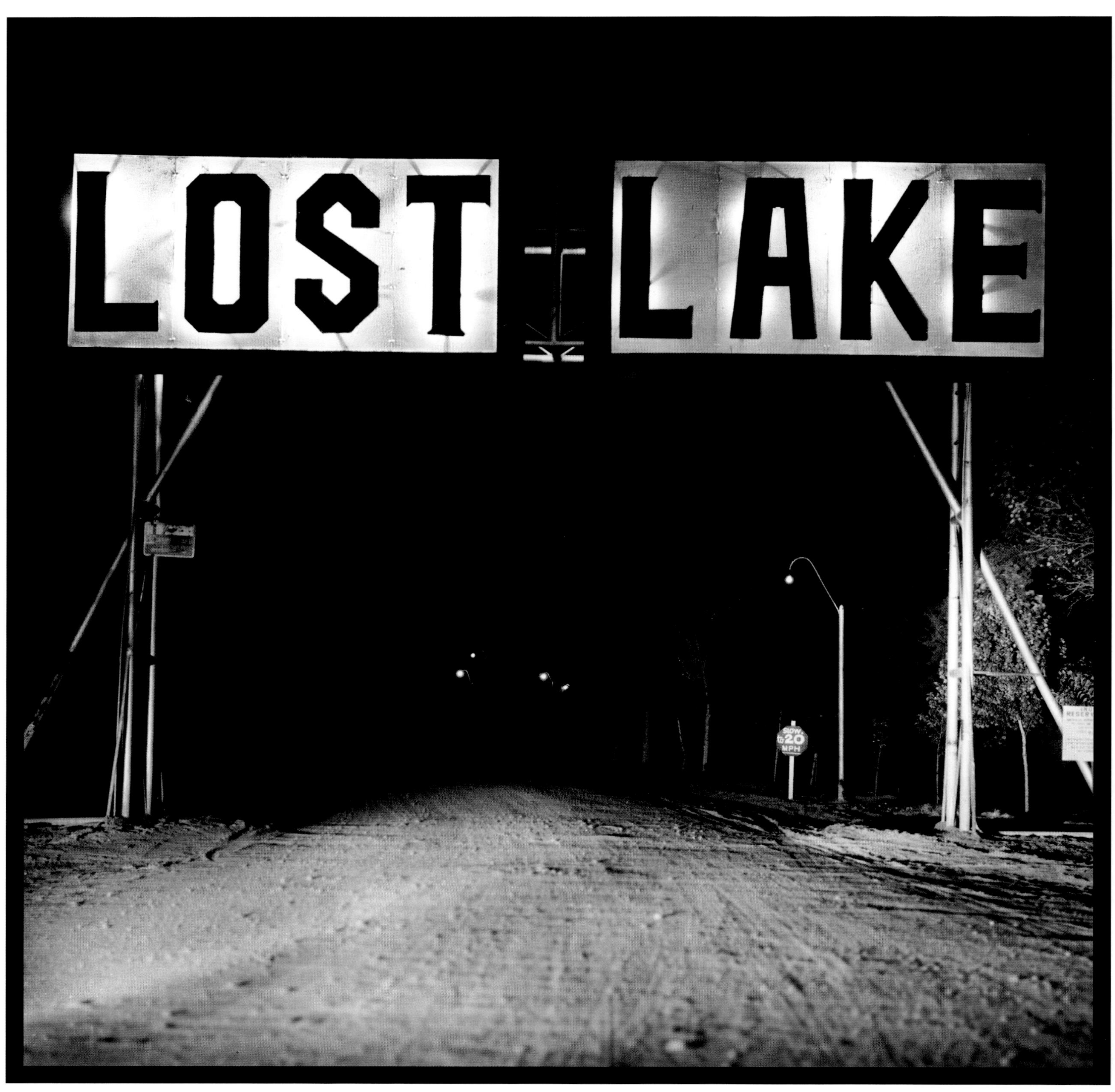
LOST
LAKE
SLOW
to 20
MPH

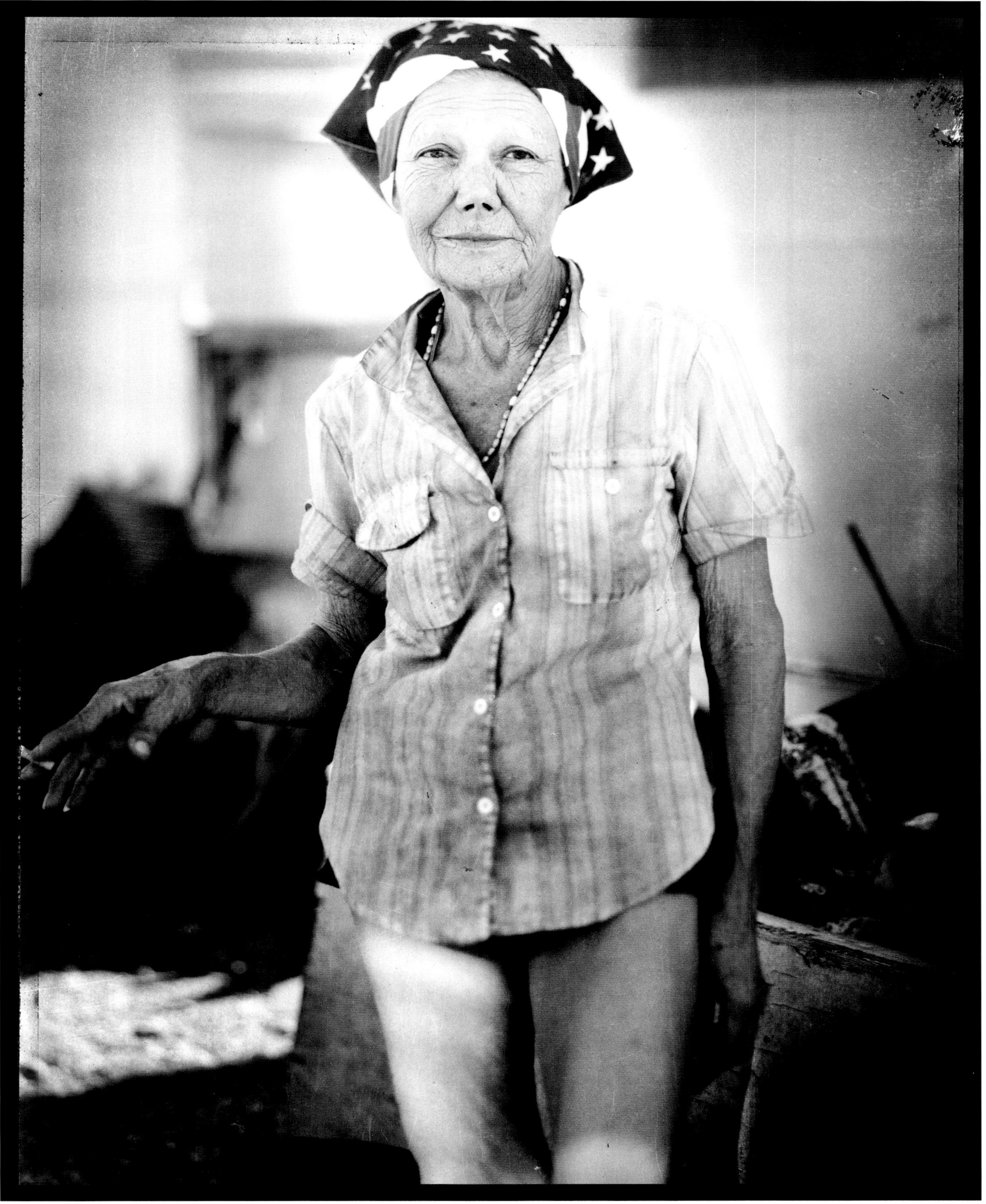

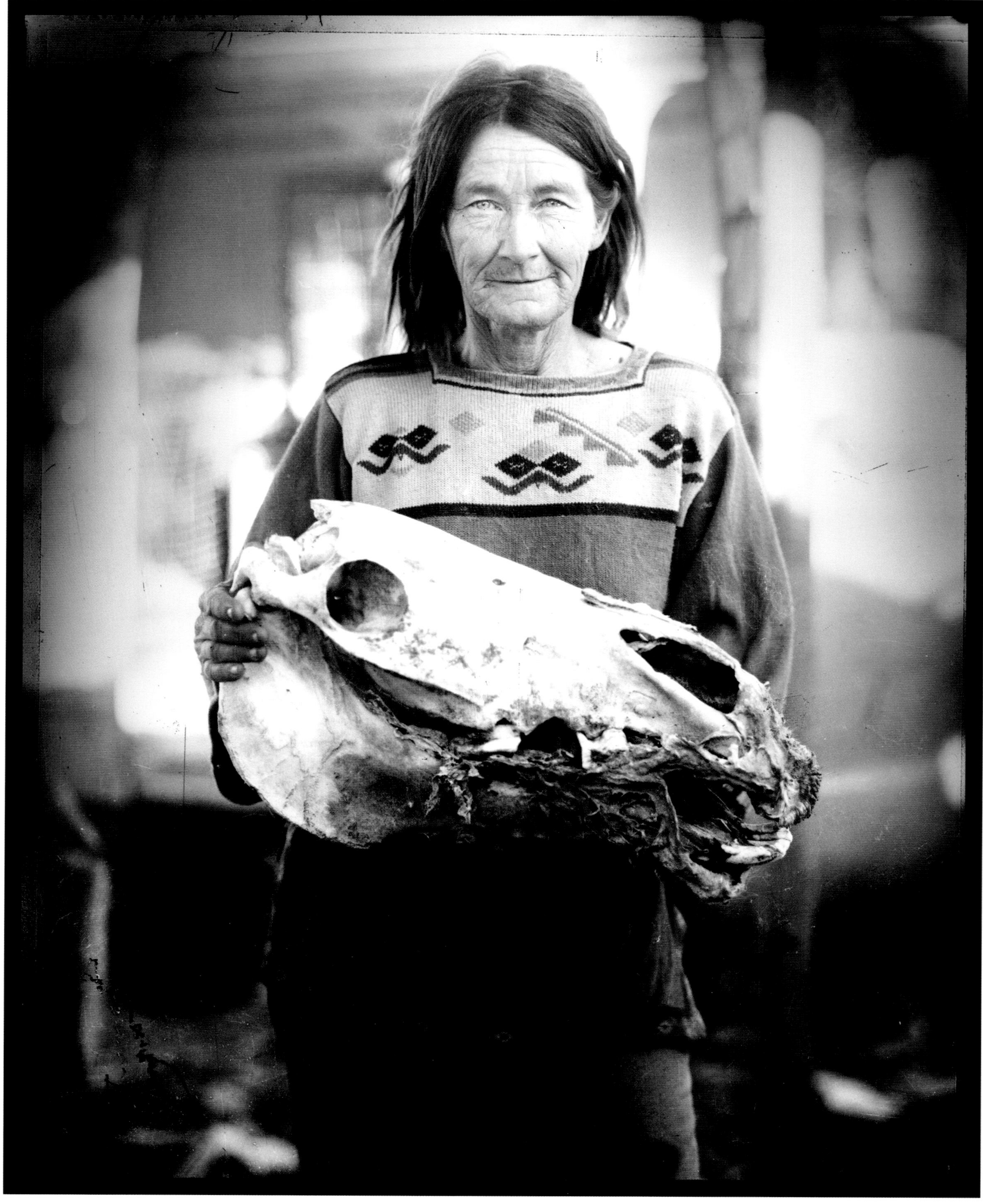

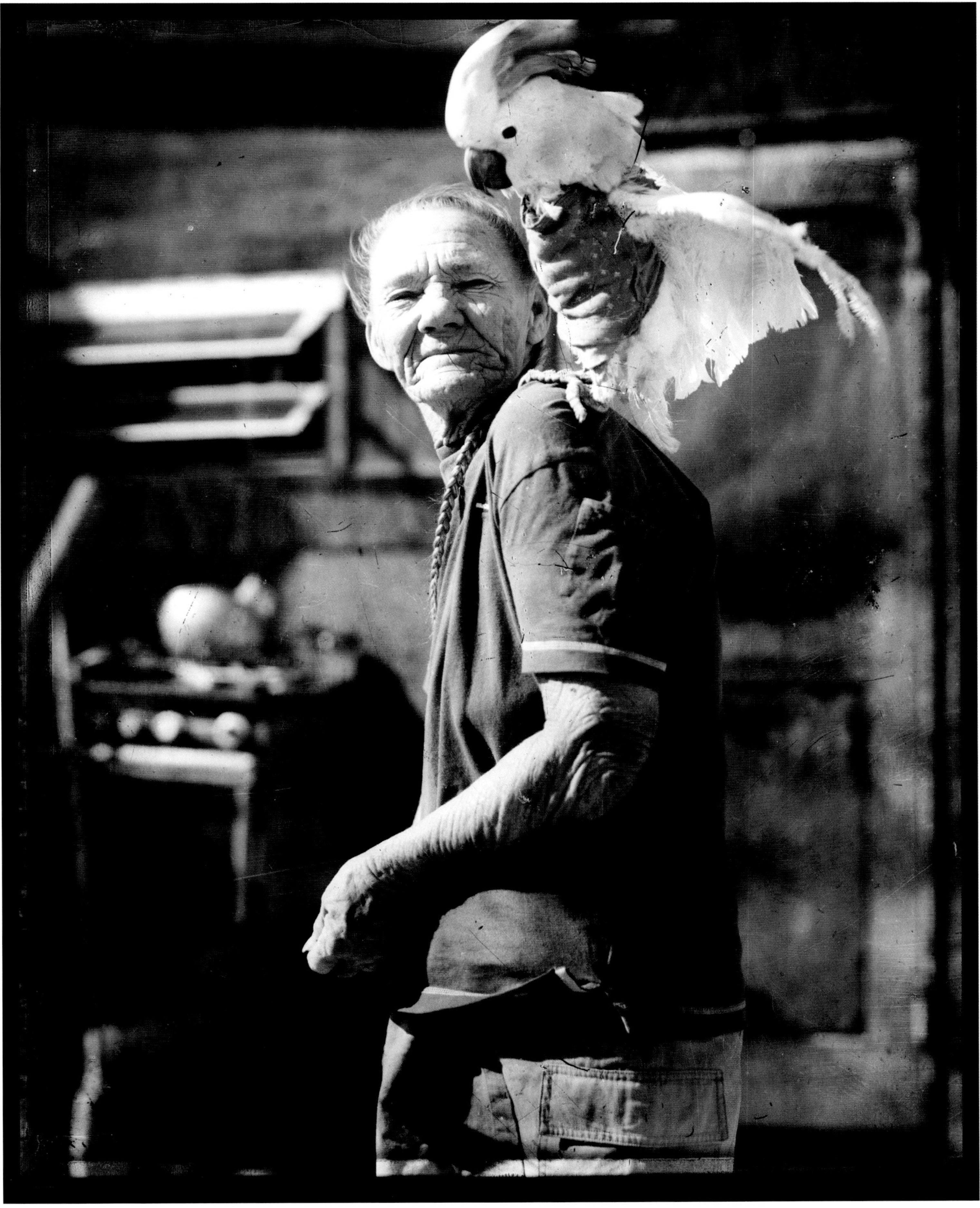

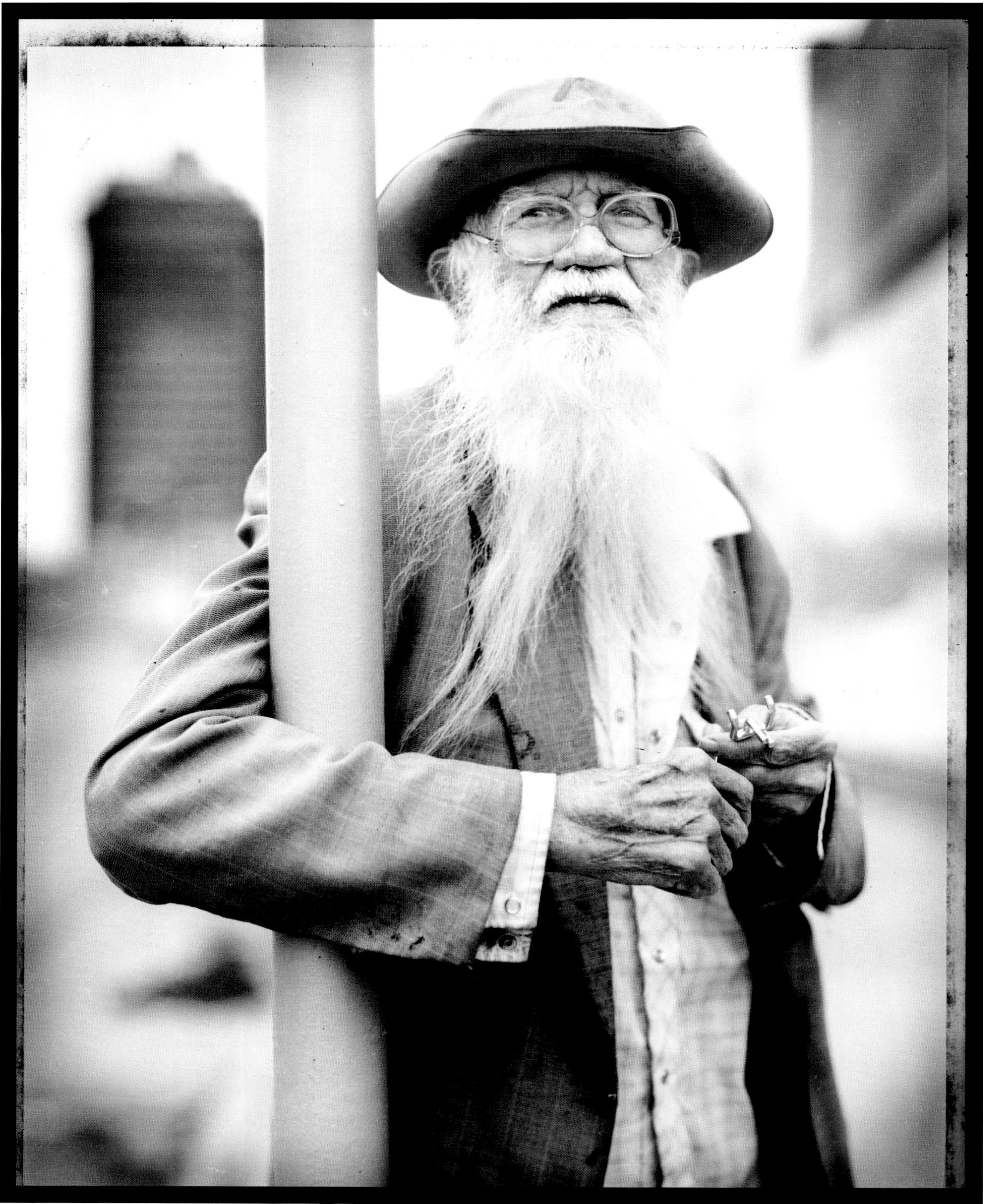

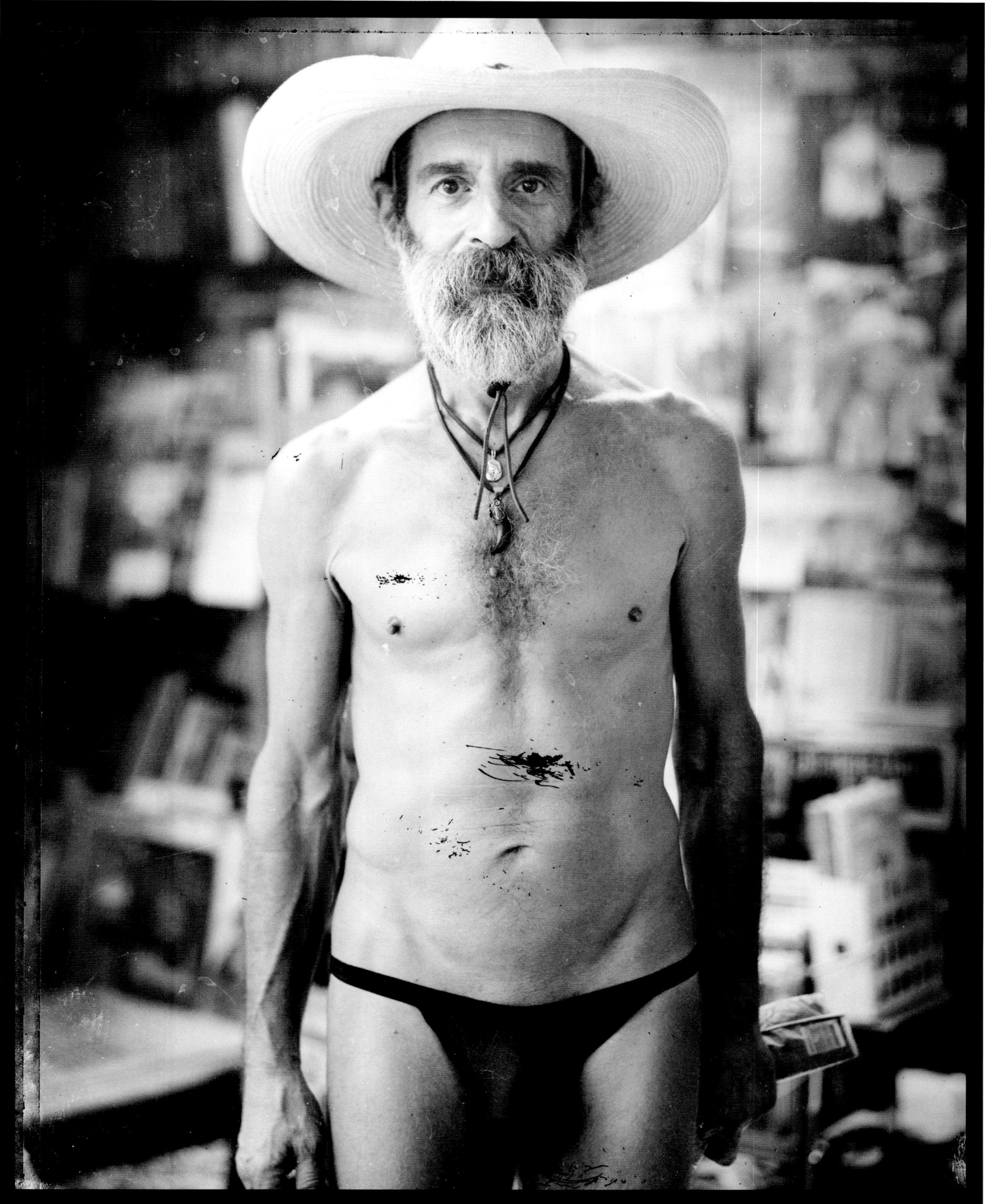

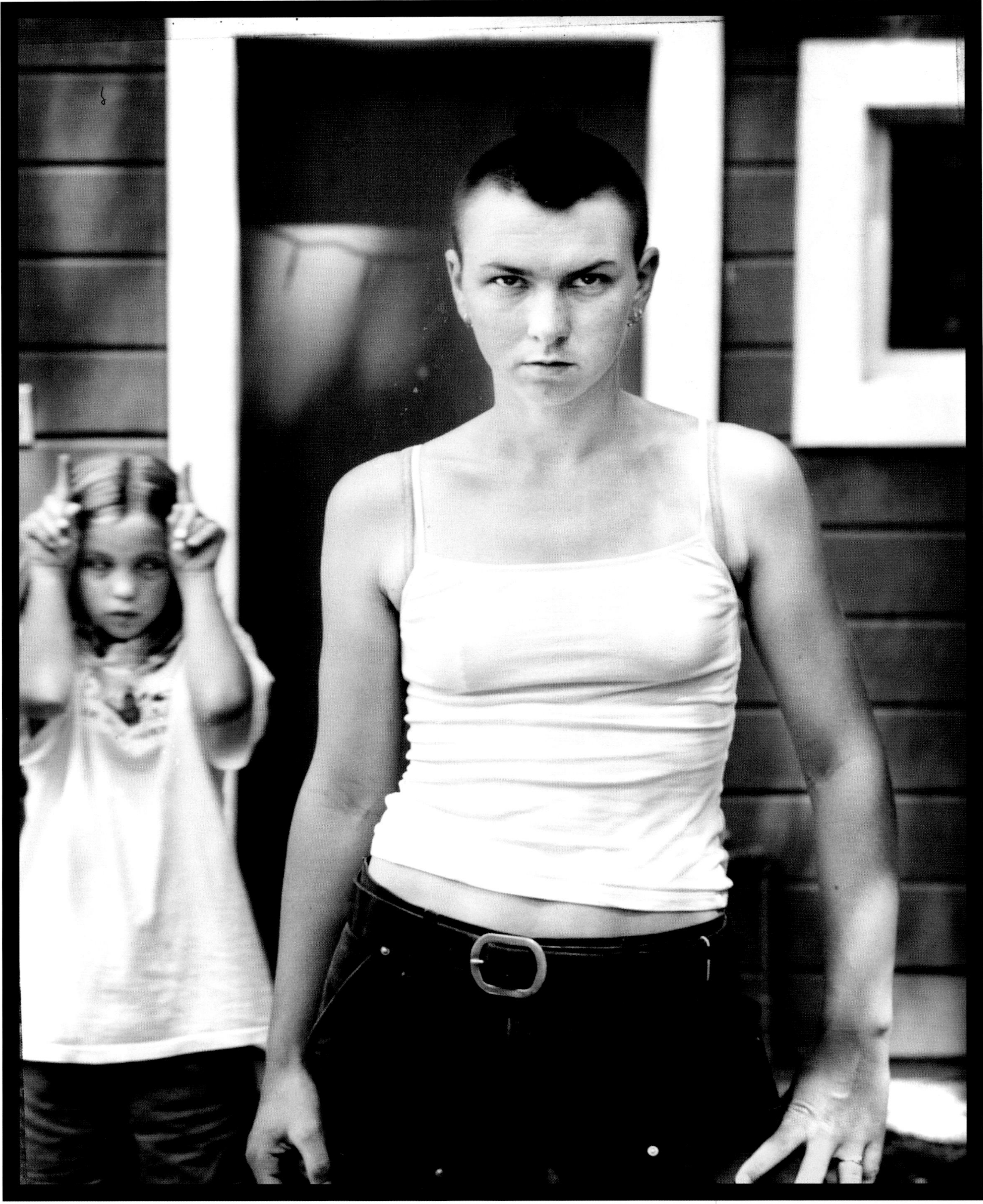

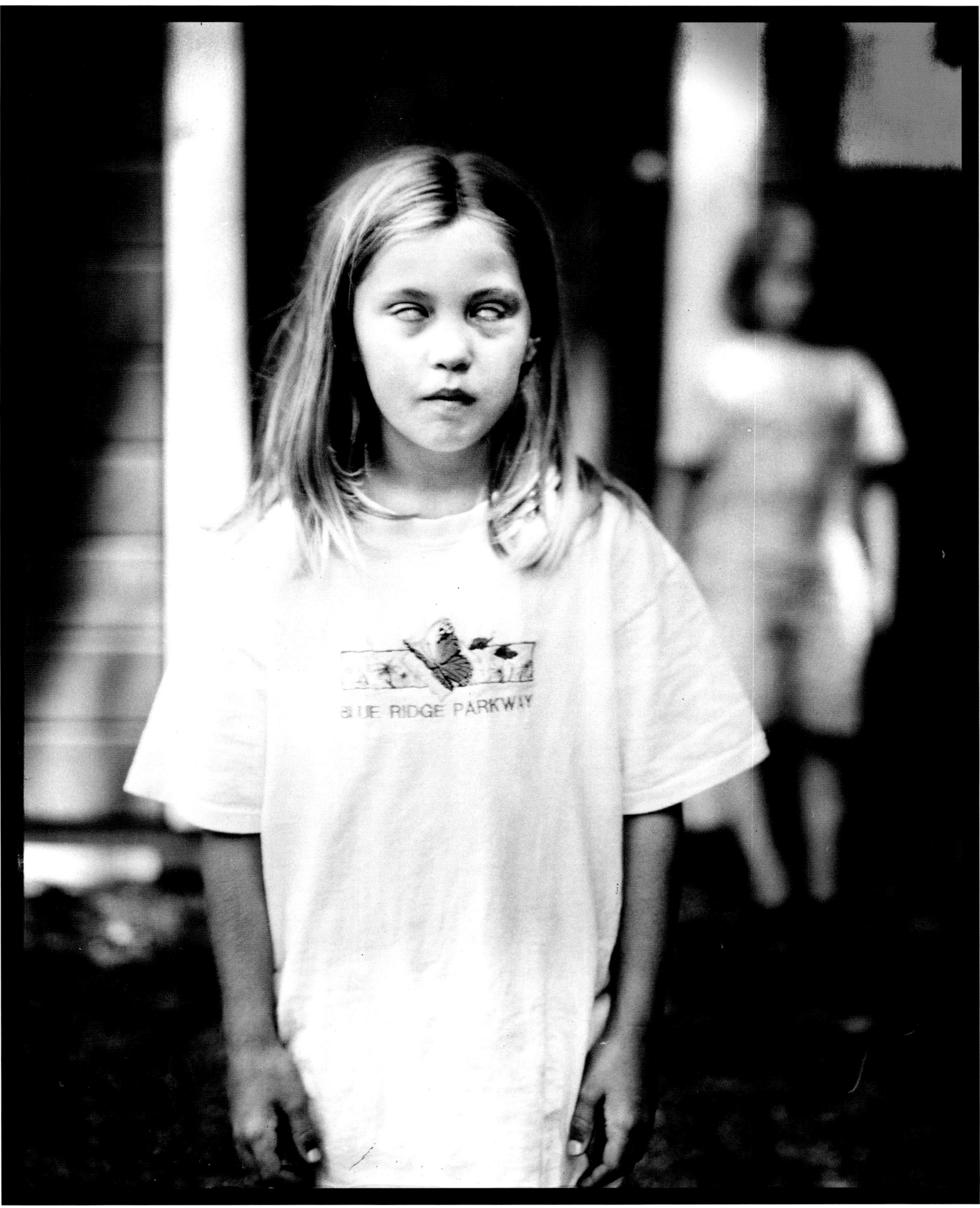
RIDGE PARKWAY

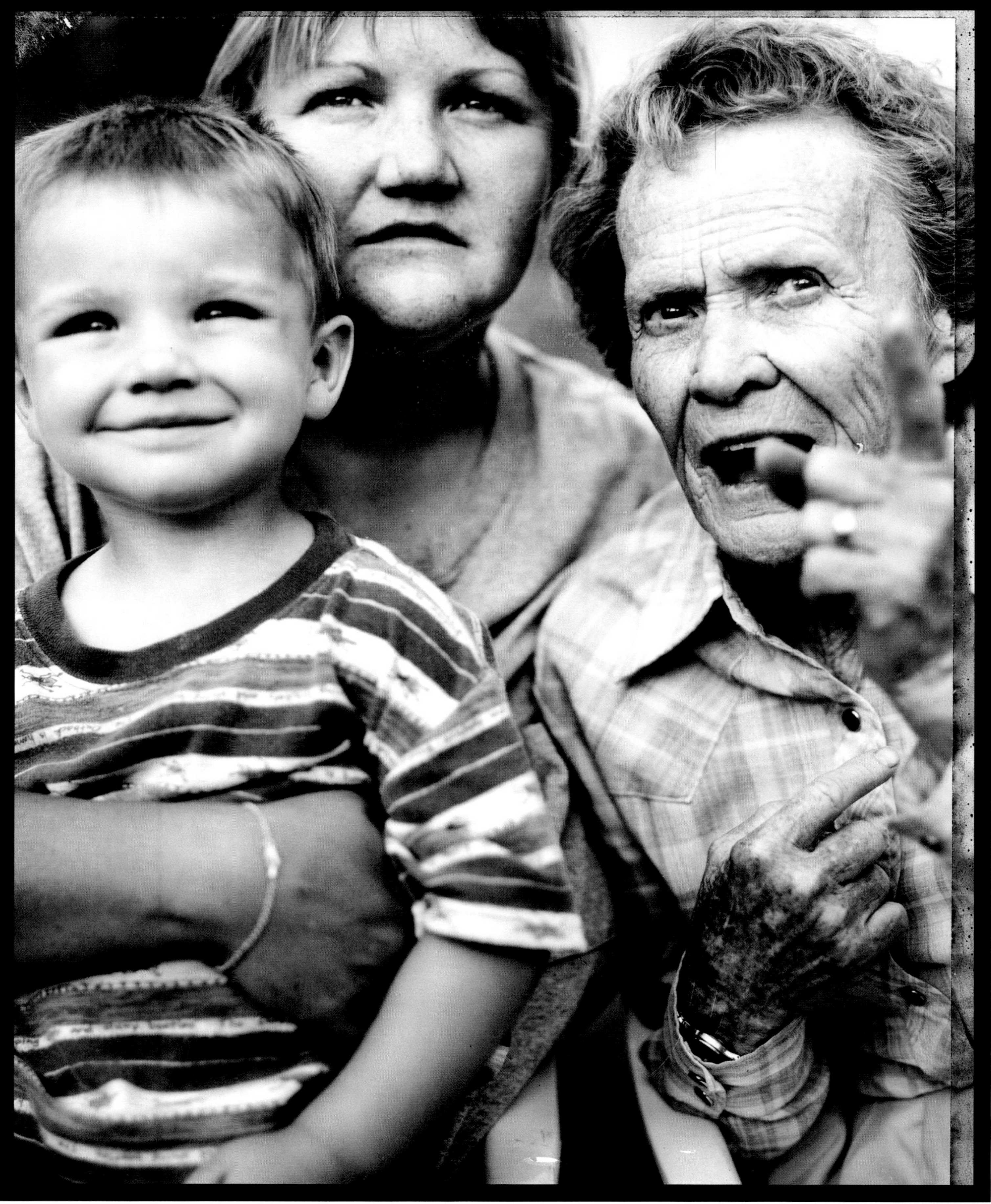

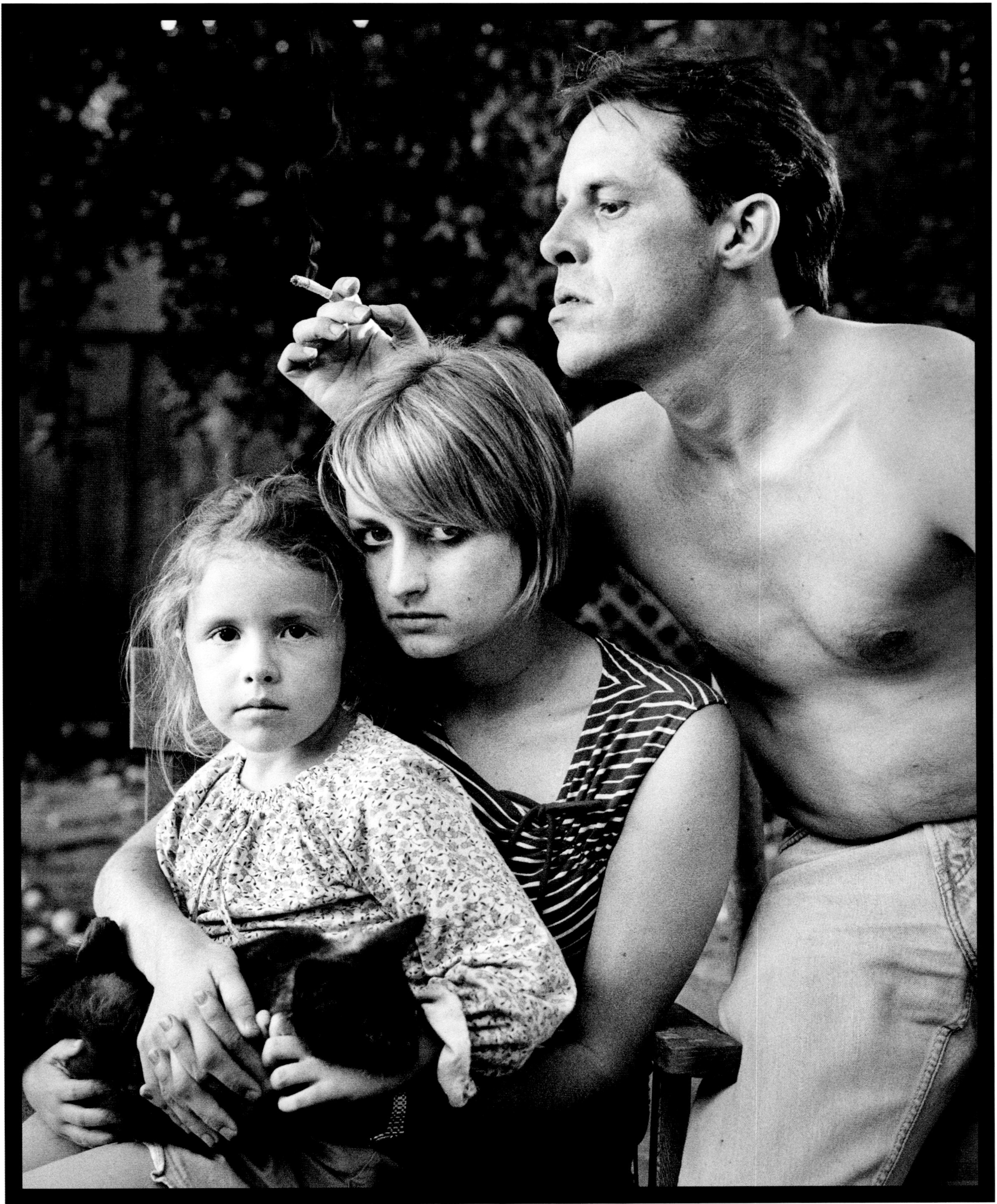

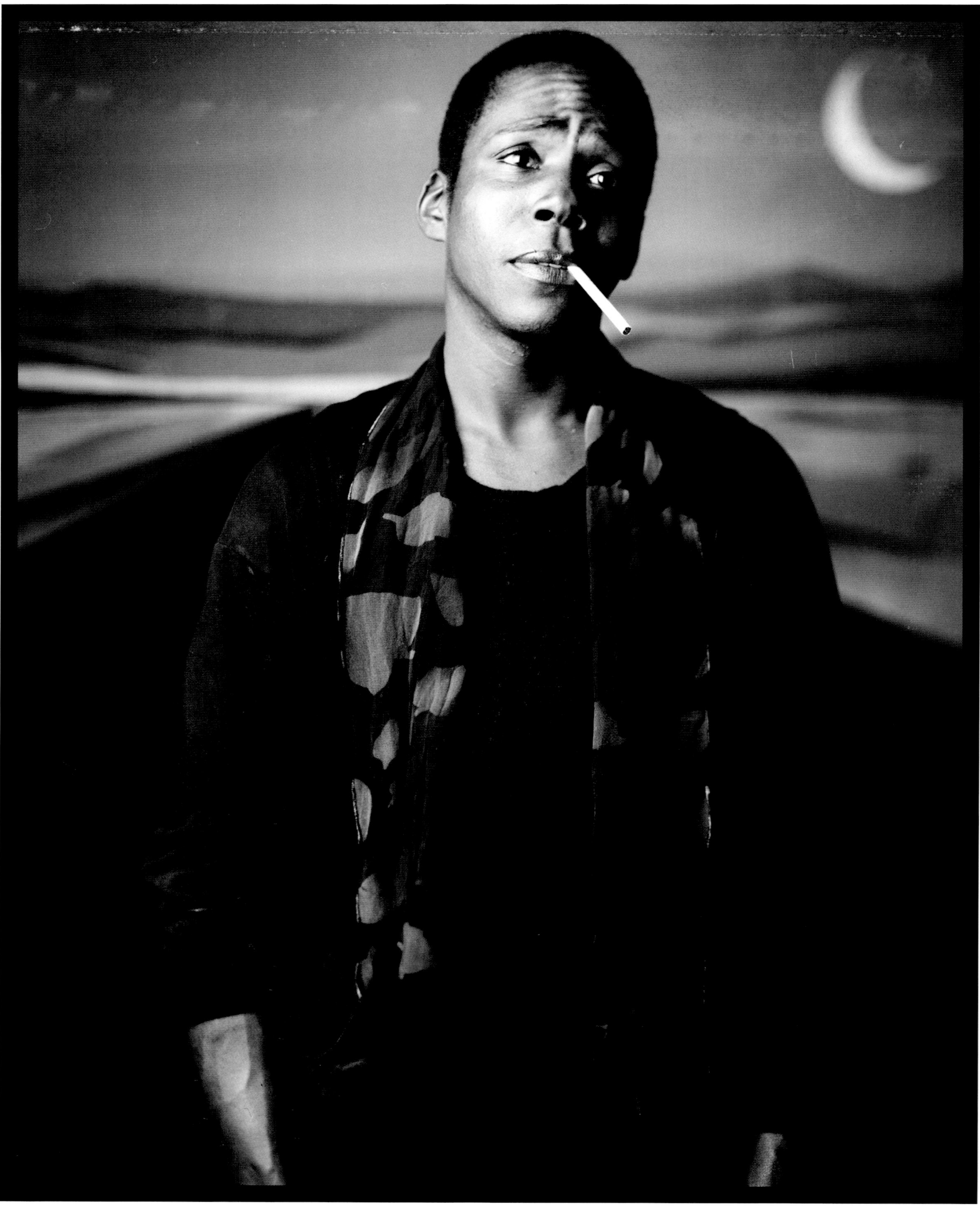

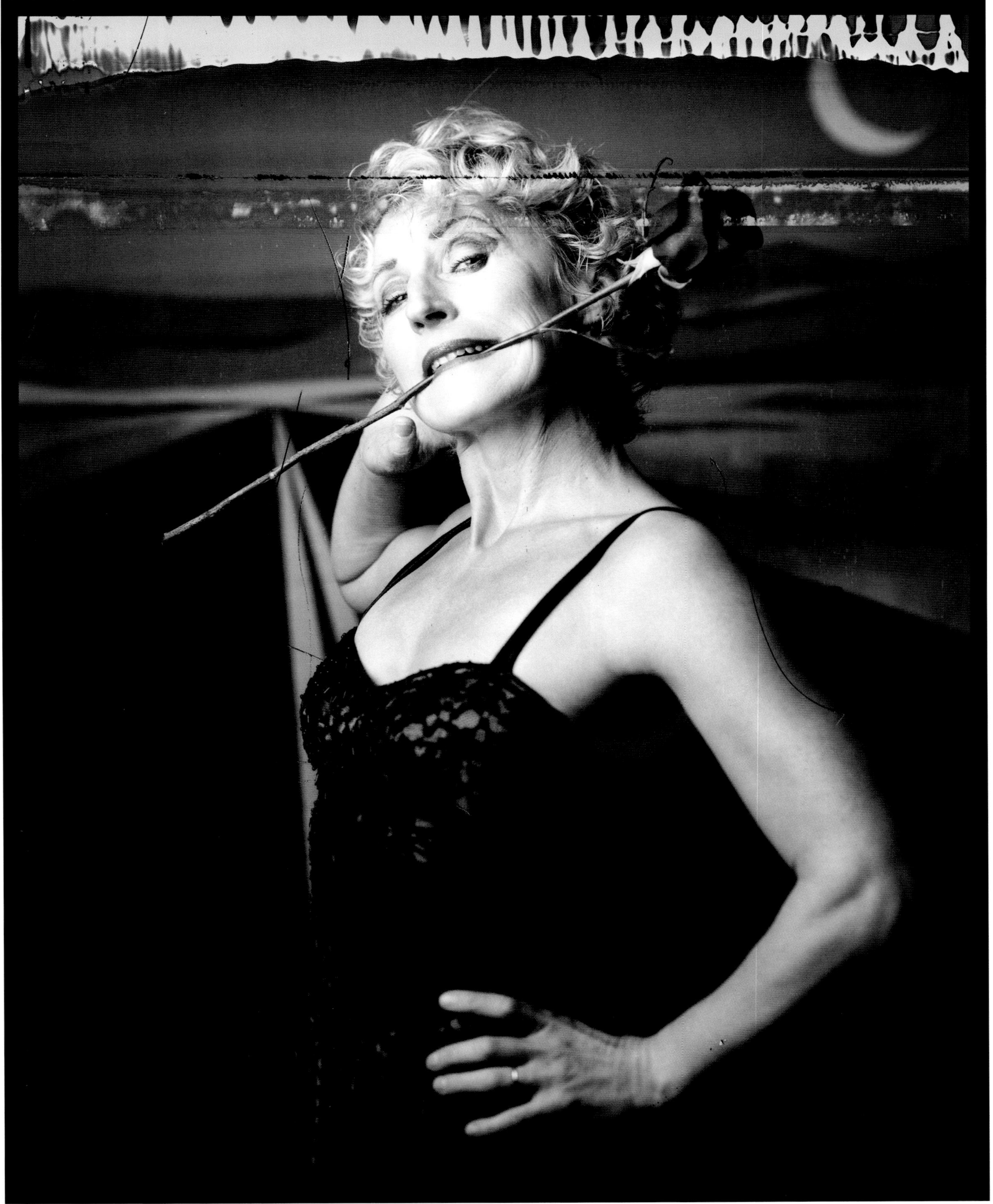

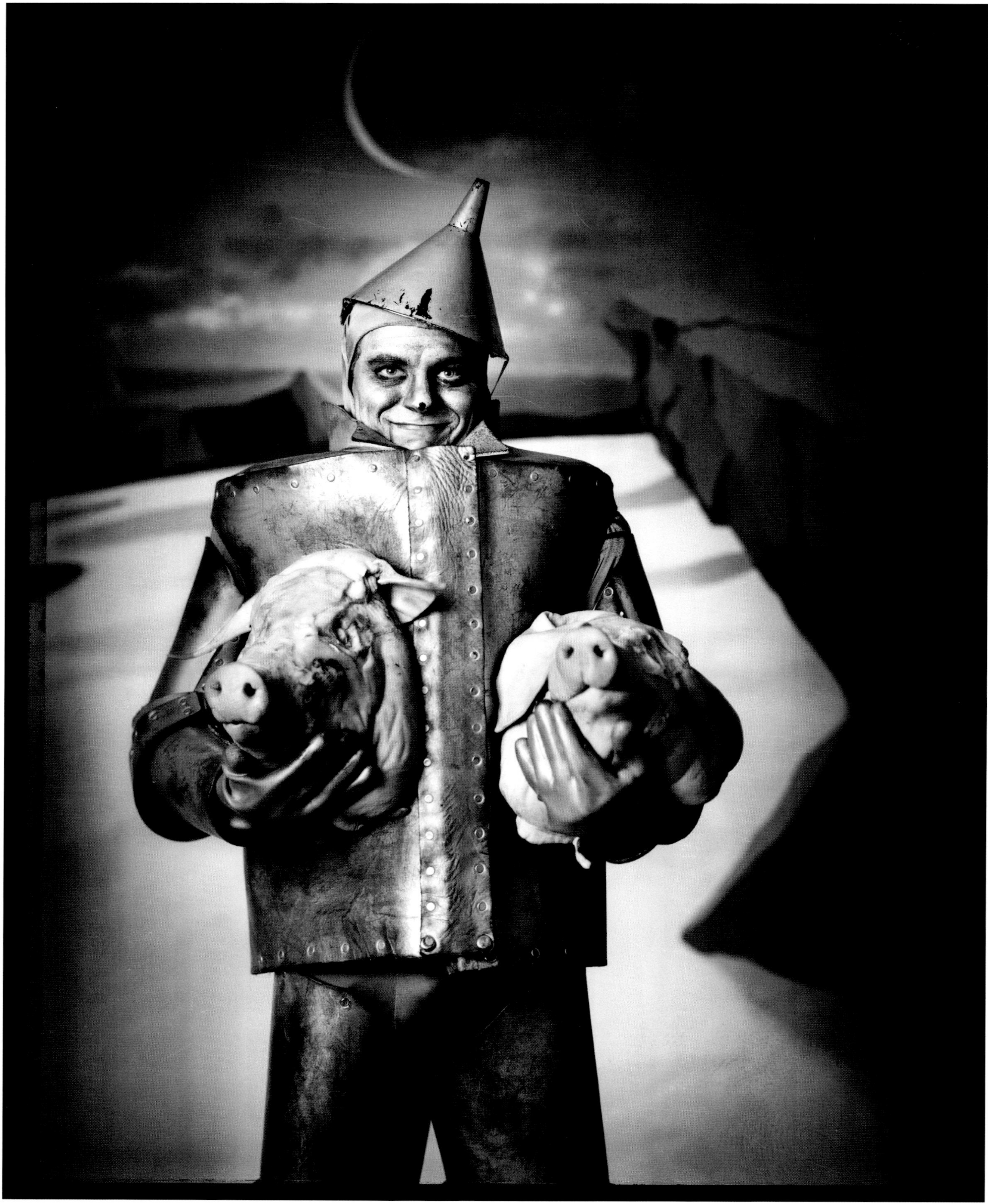

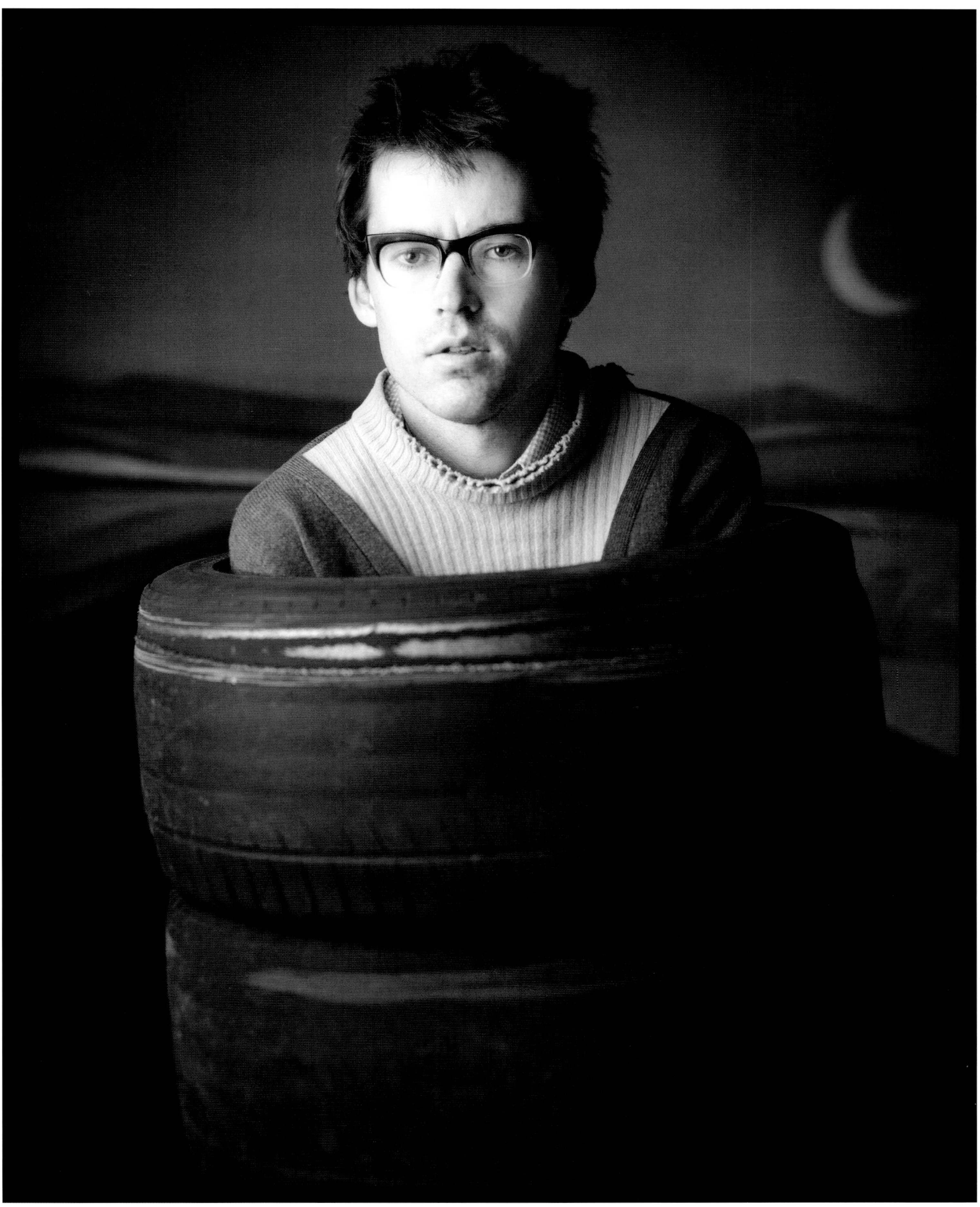

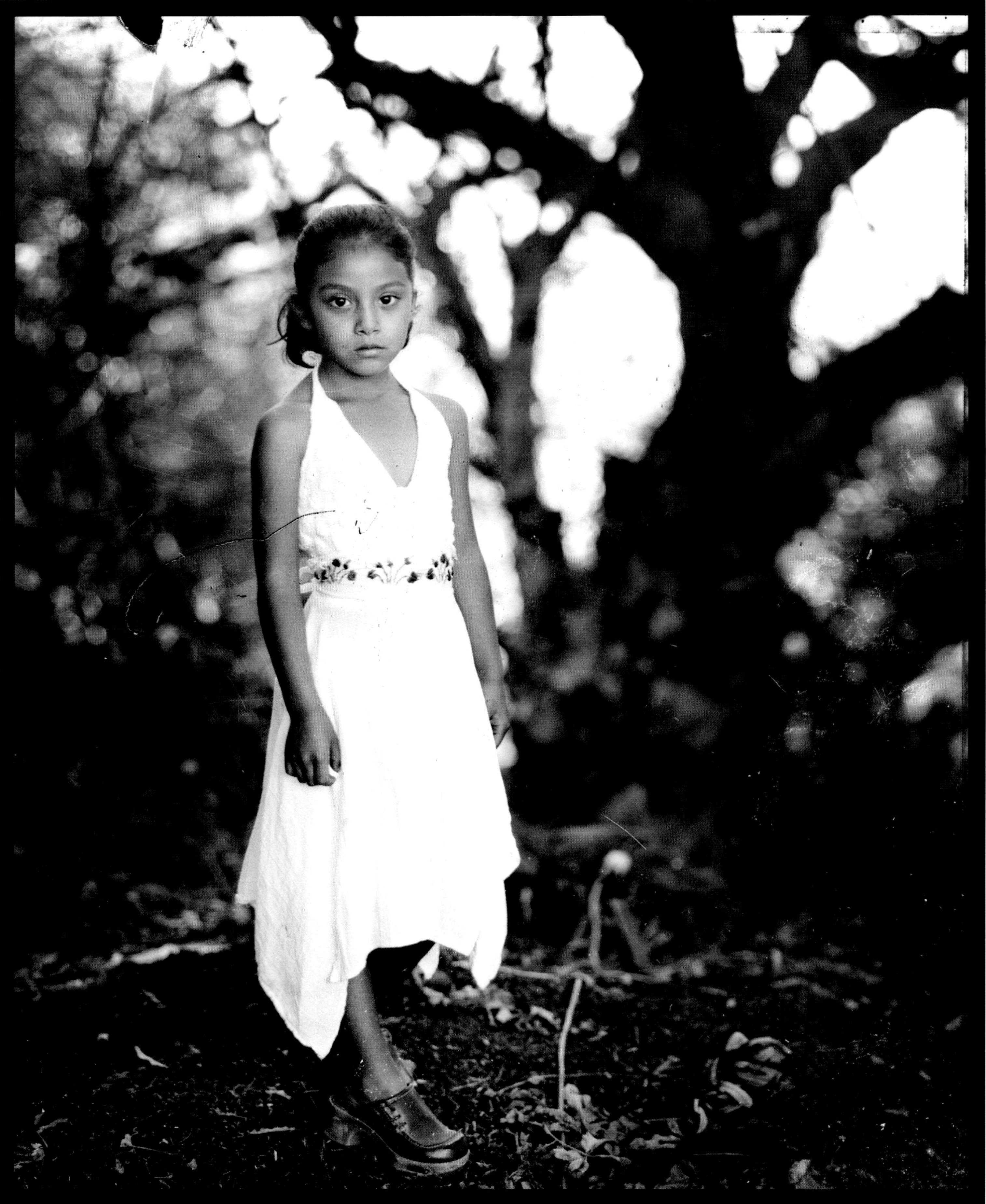

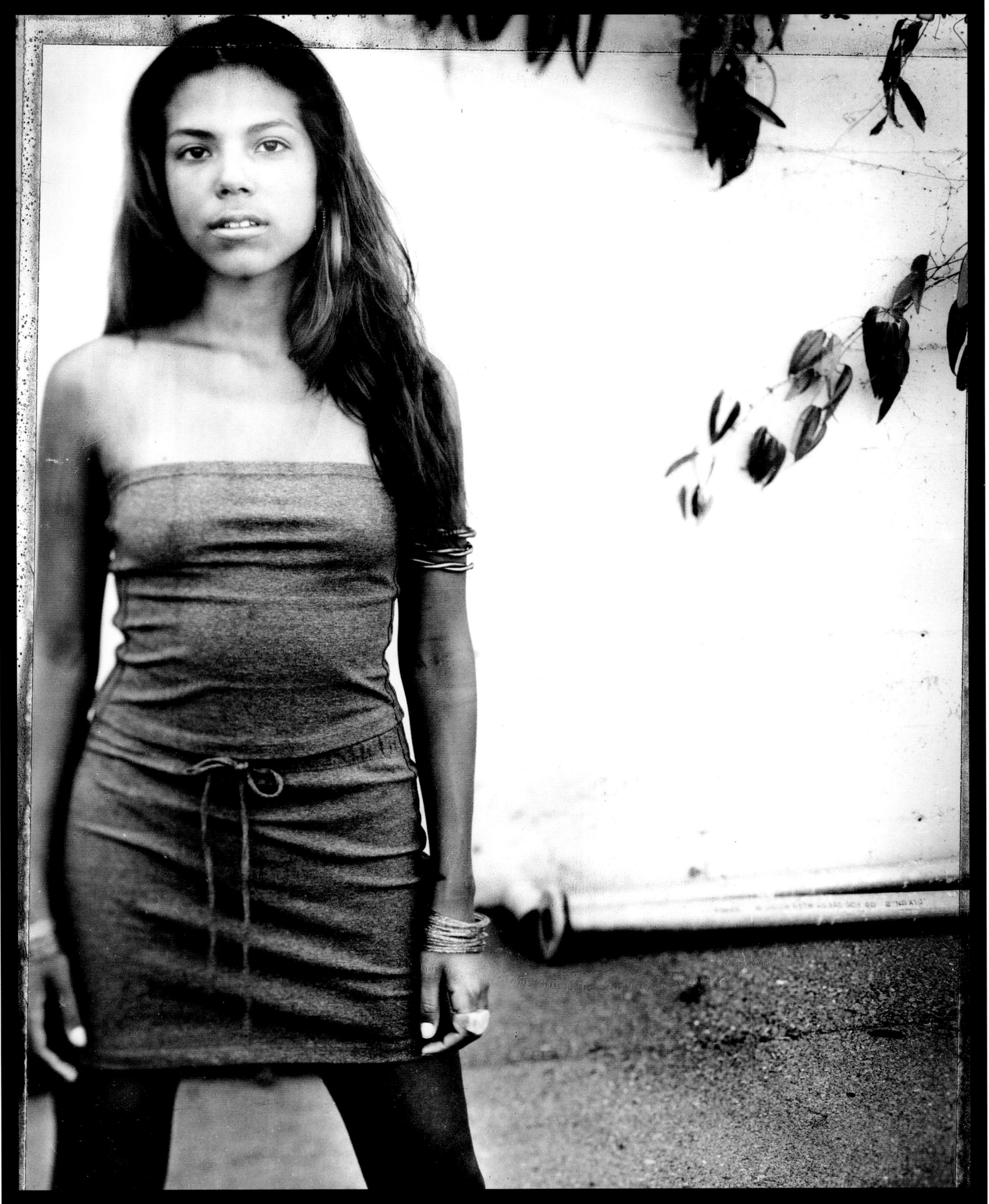

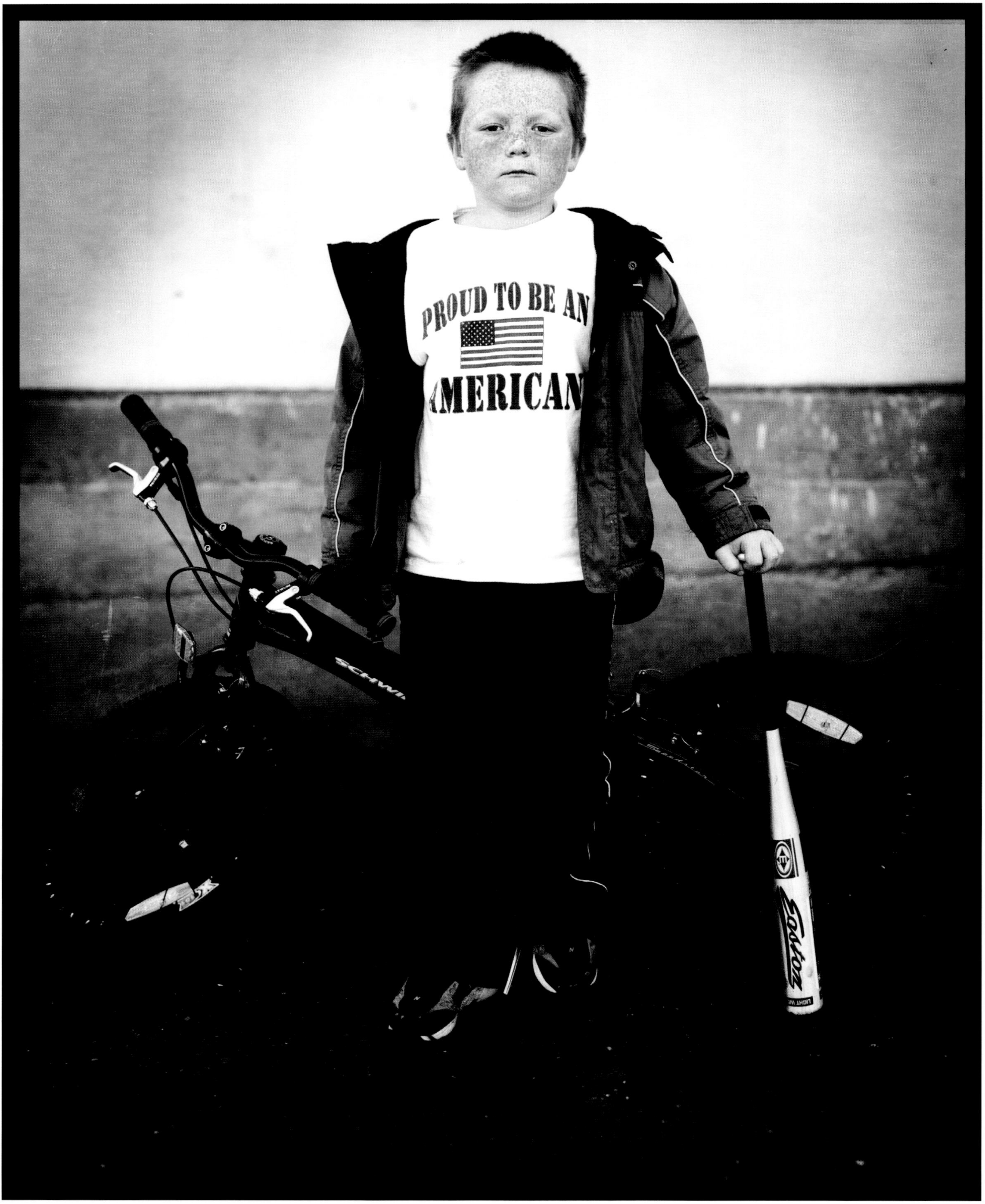
PROUD TO BE AN
AMERICAN

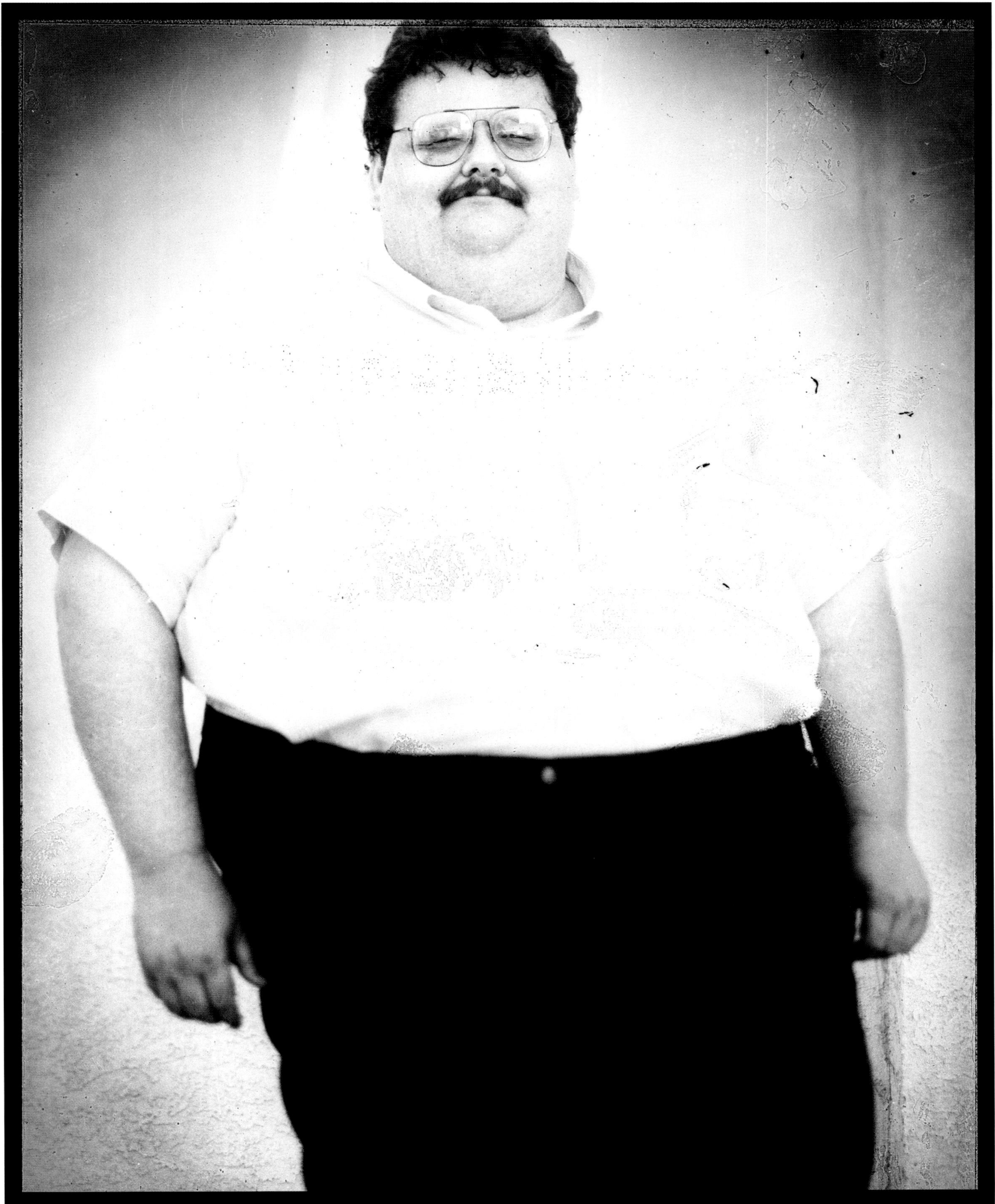

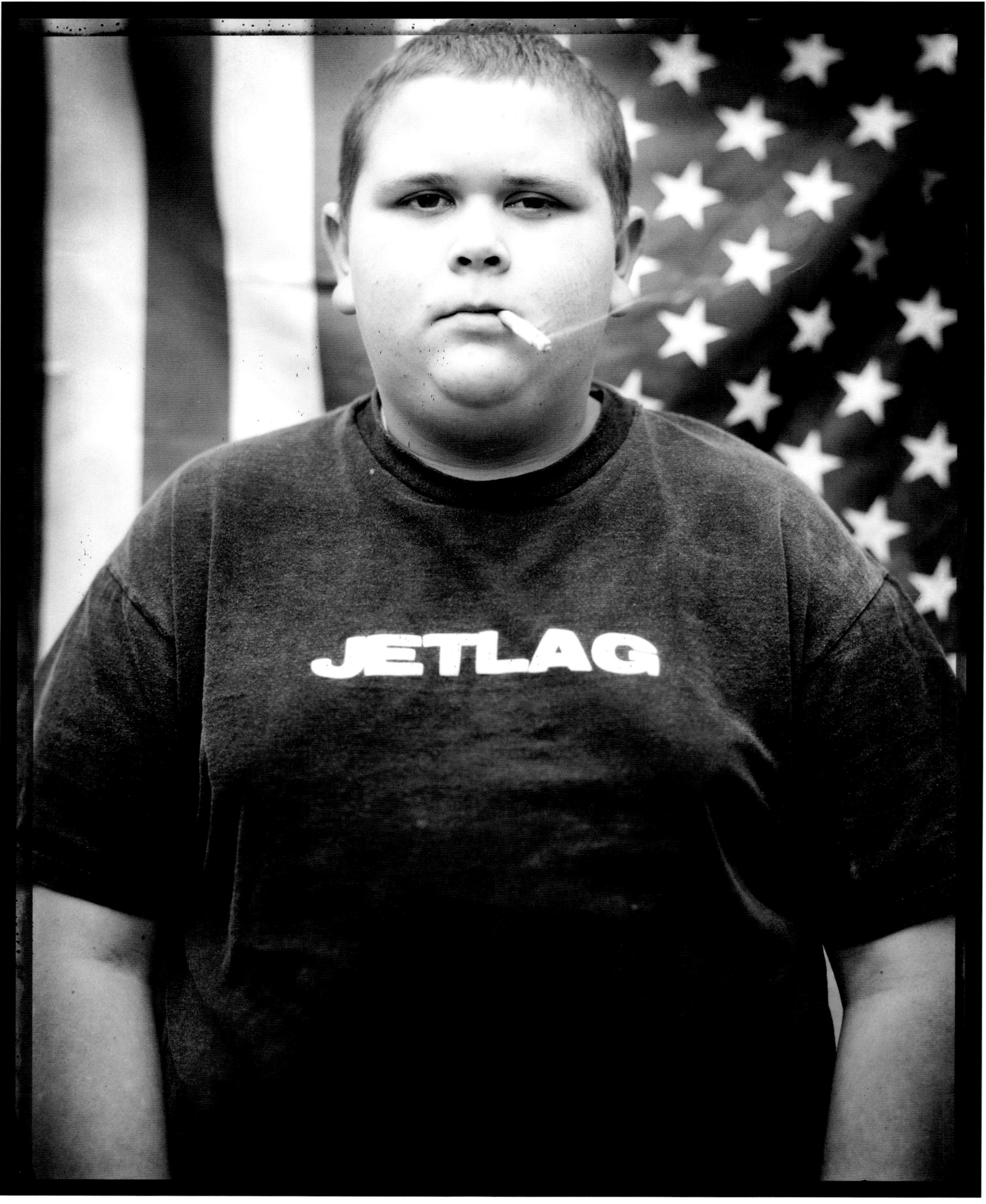
JETLAG

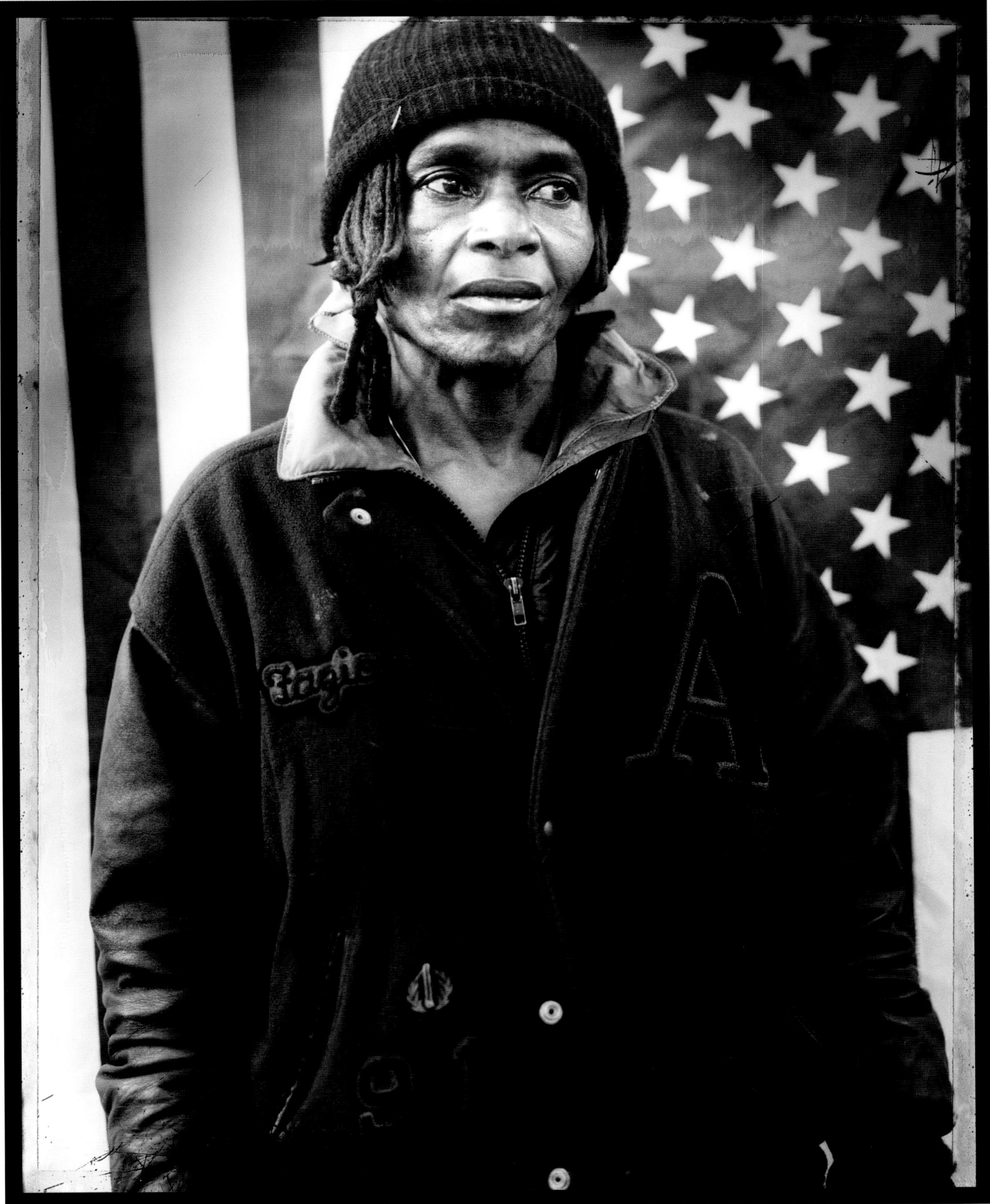
A

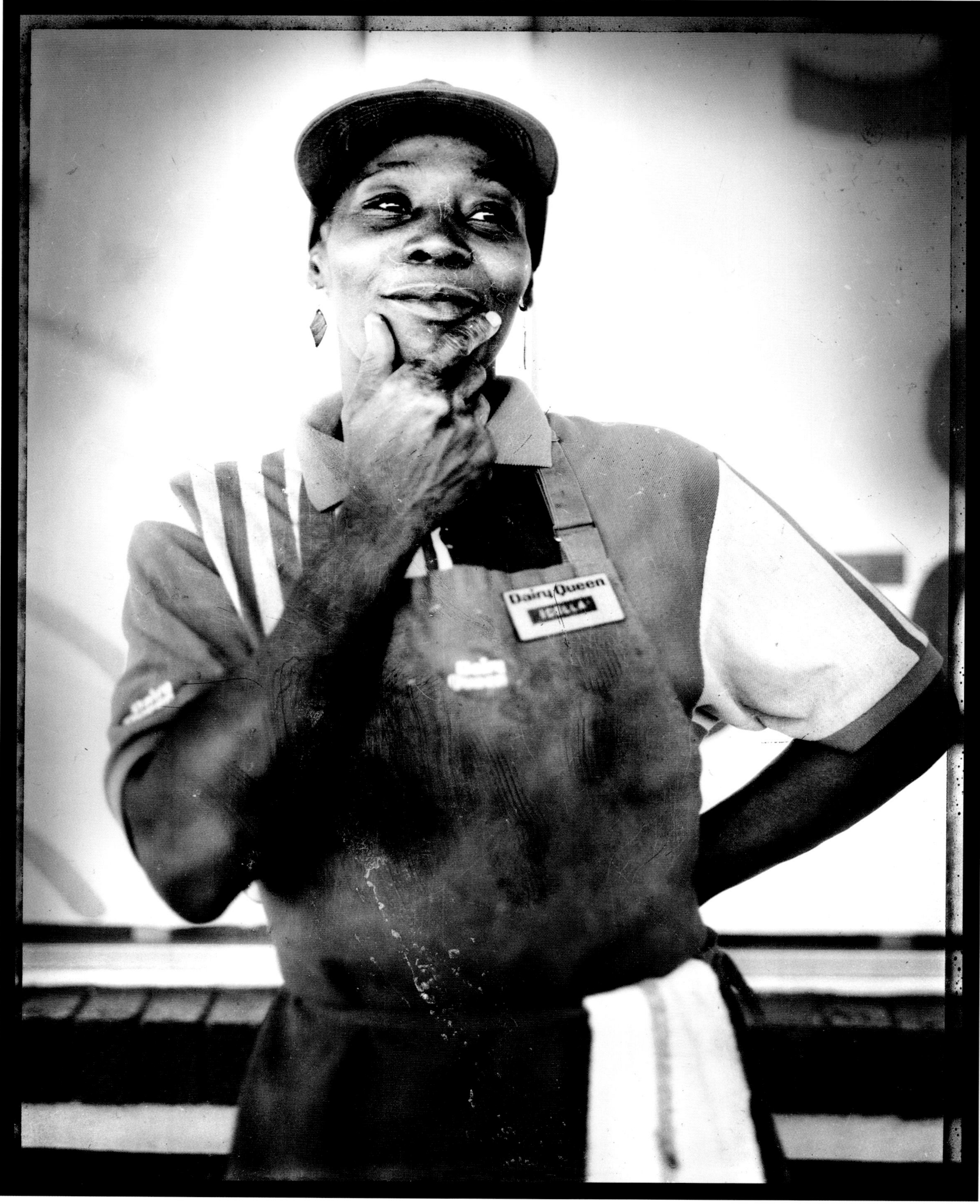
Dairy Queen

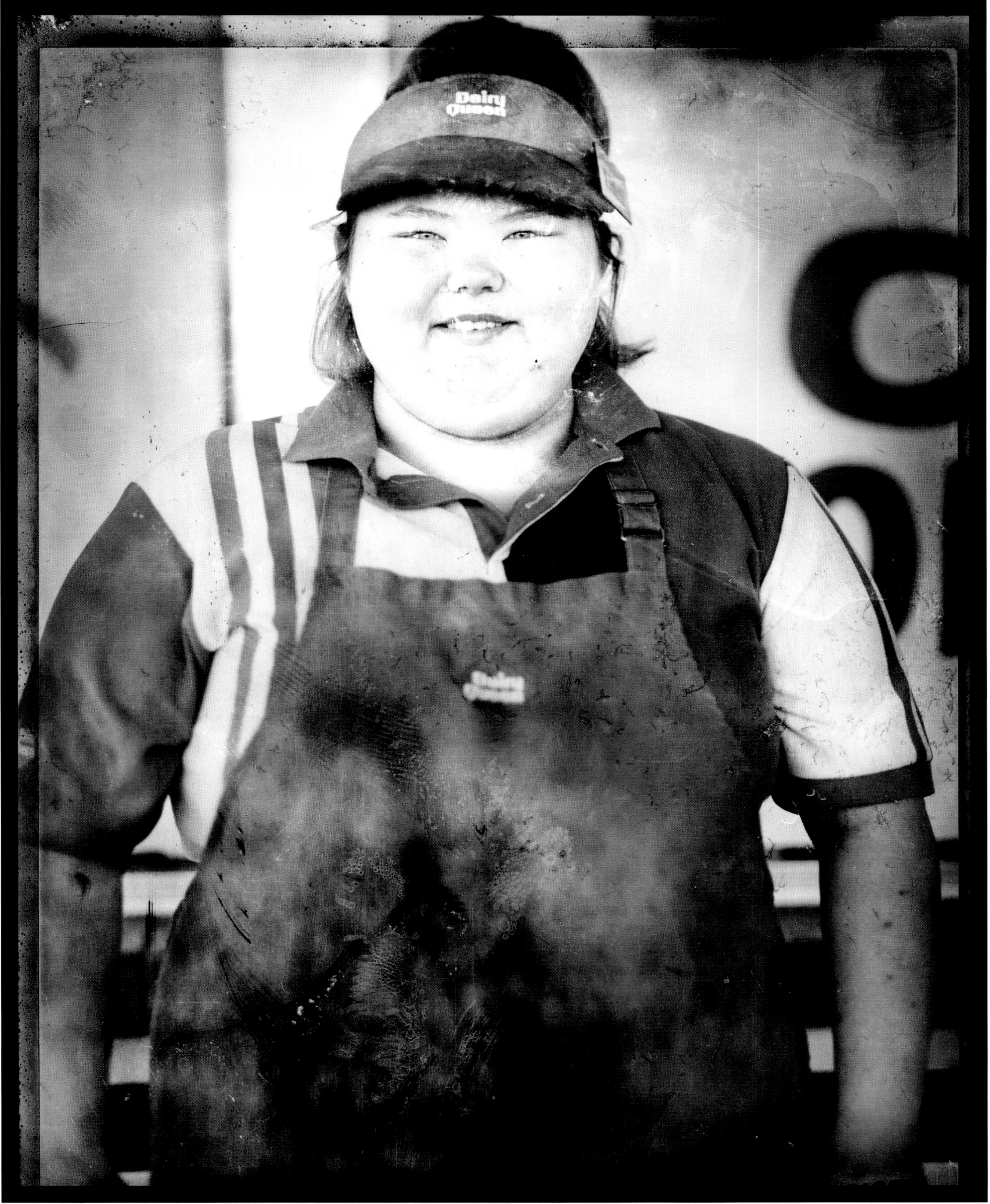
Dairy
Queen

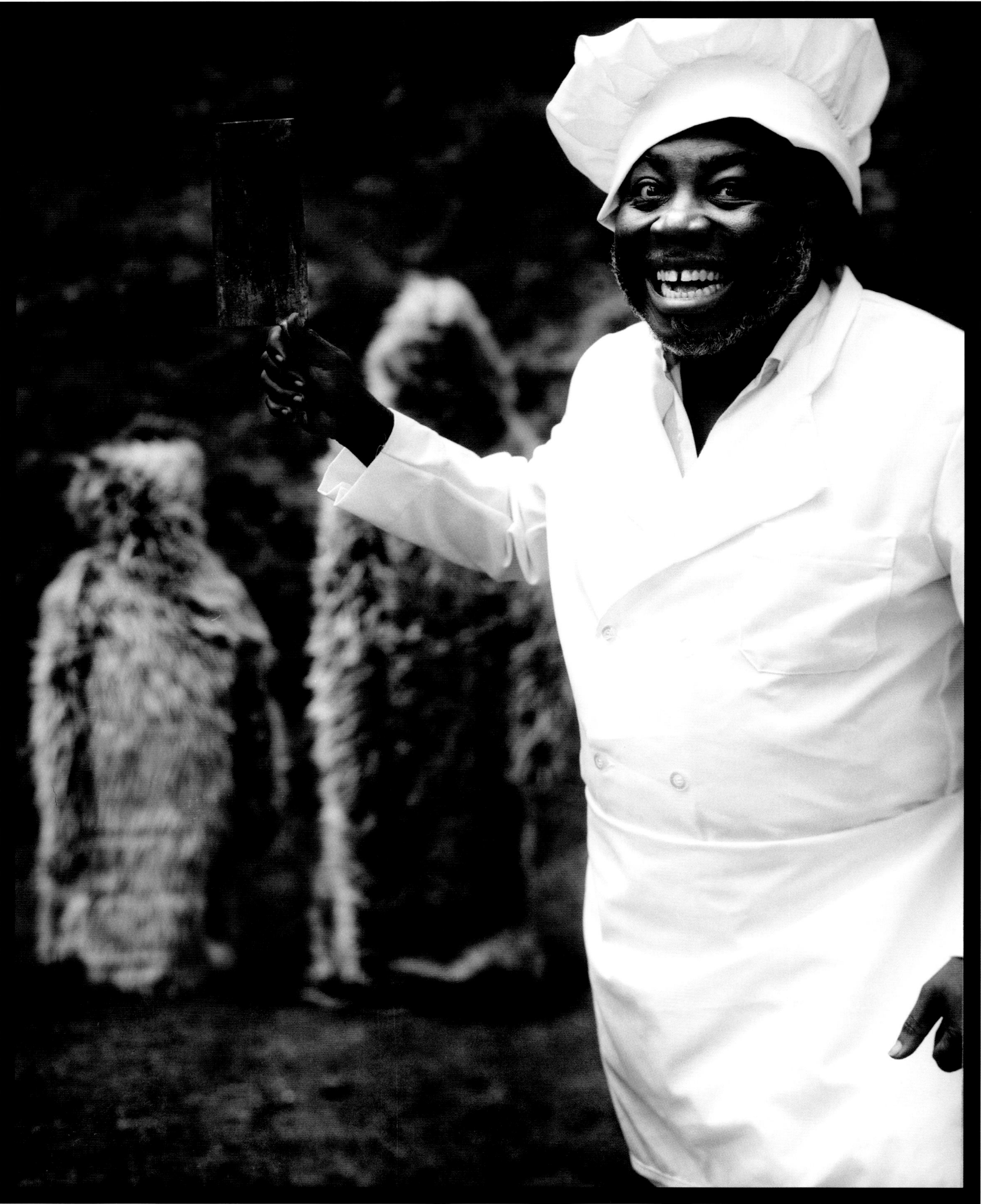

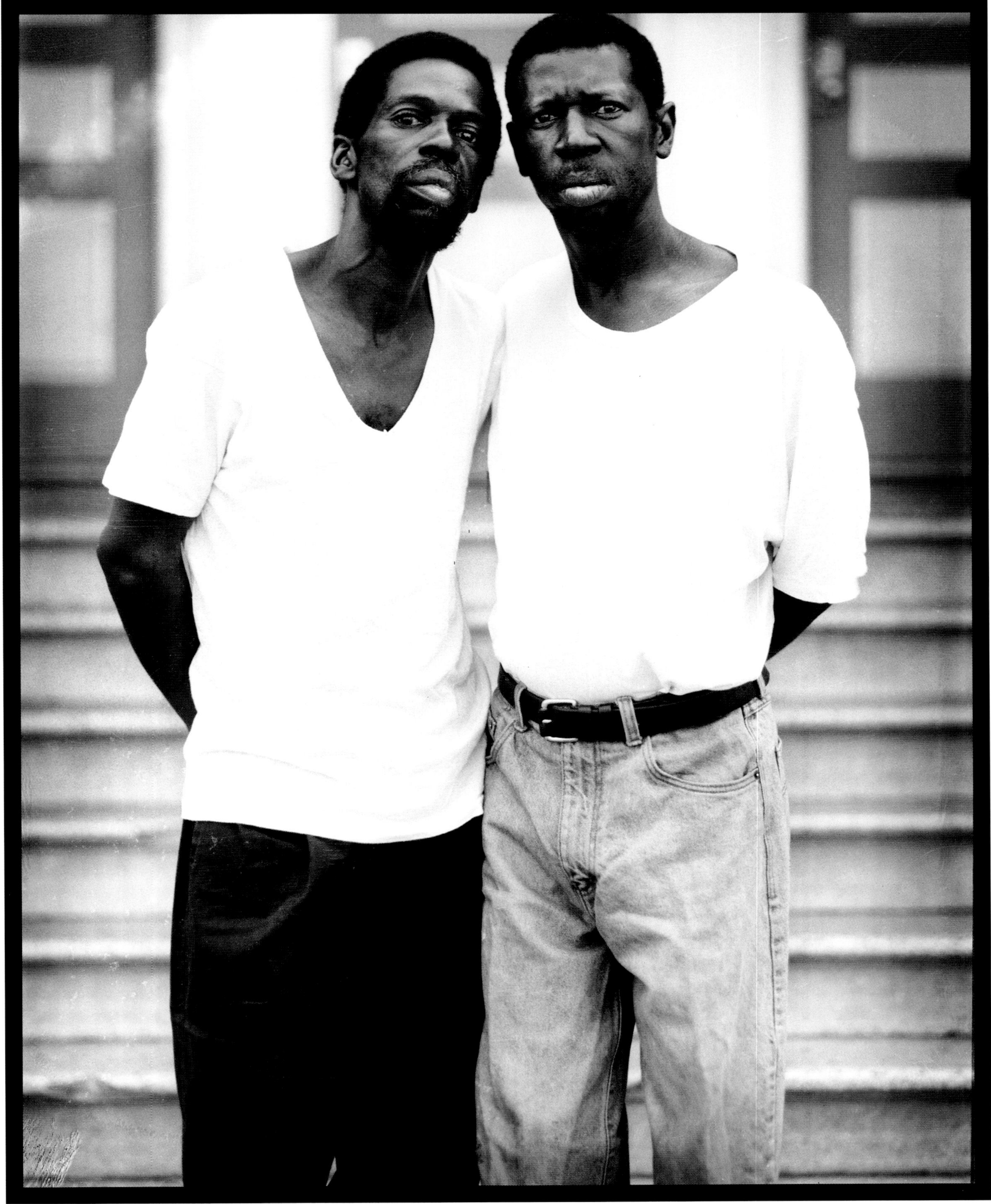

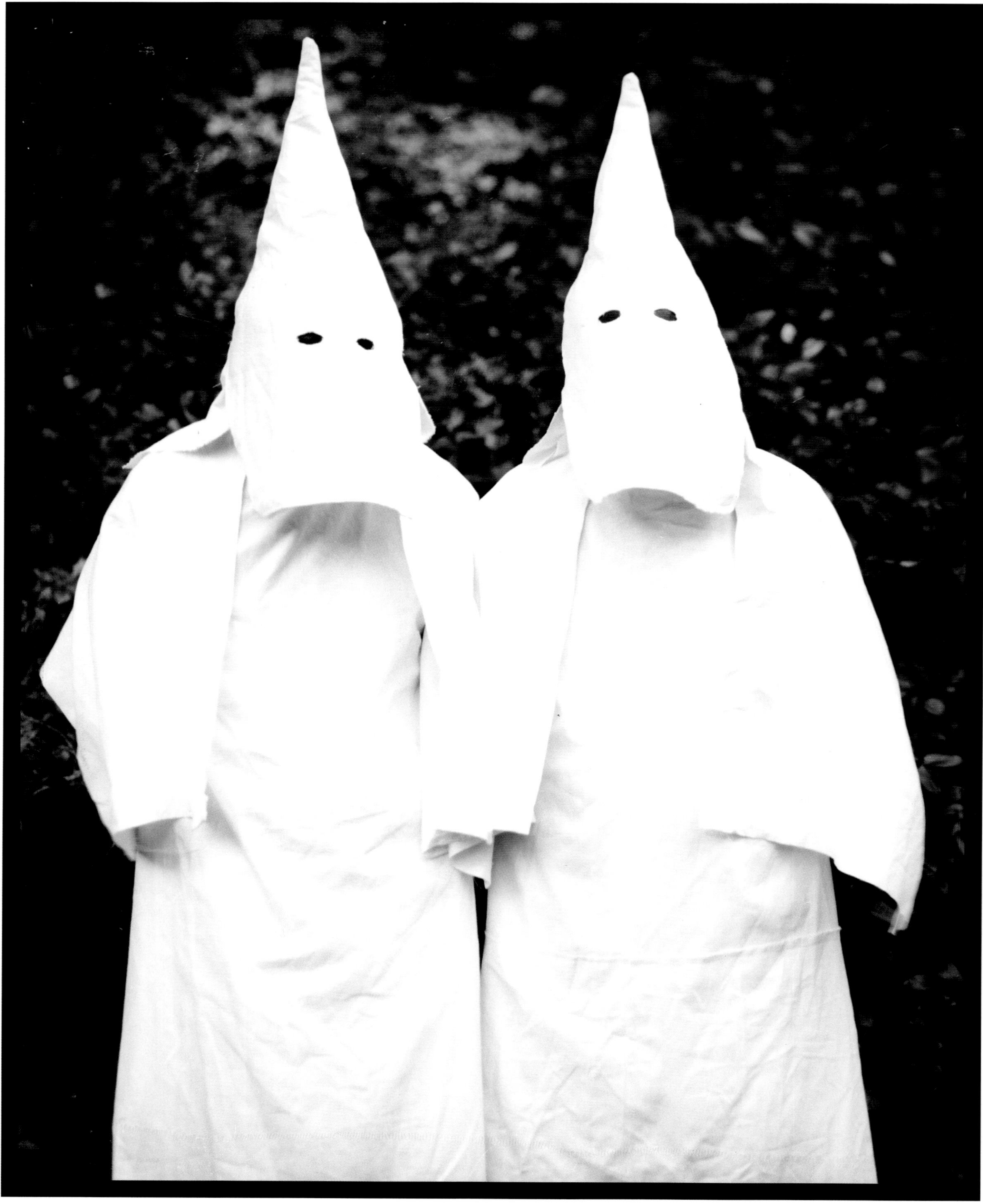

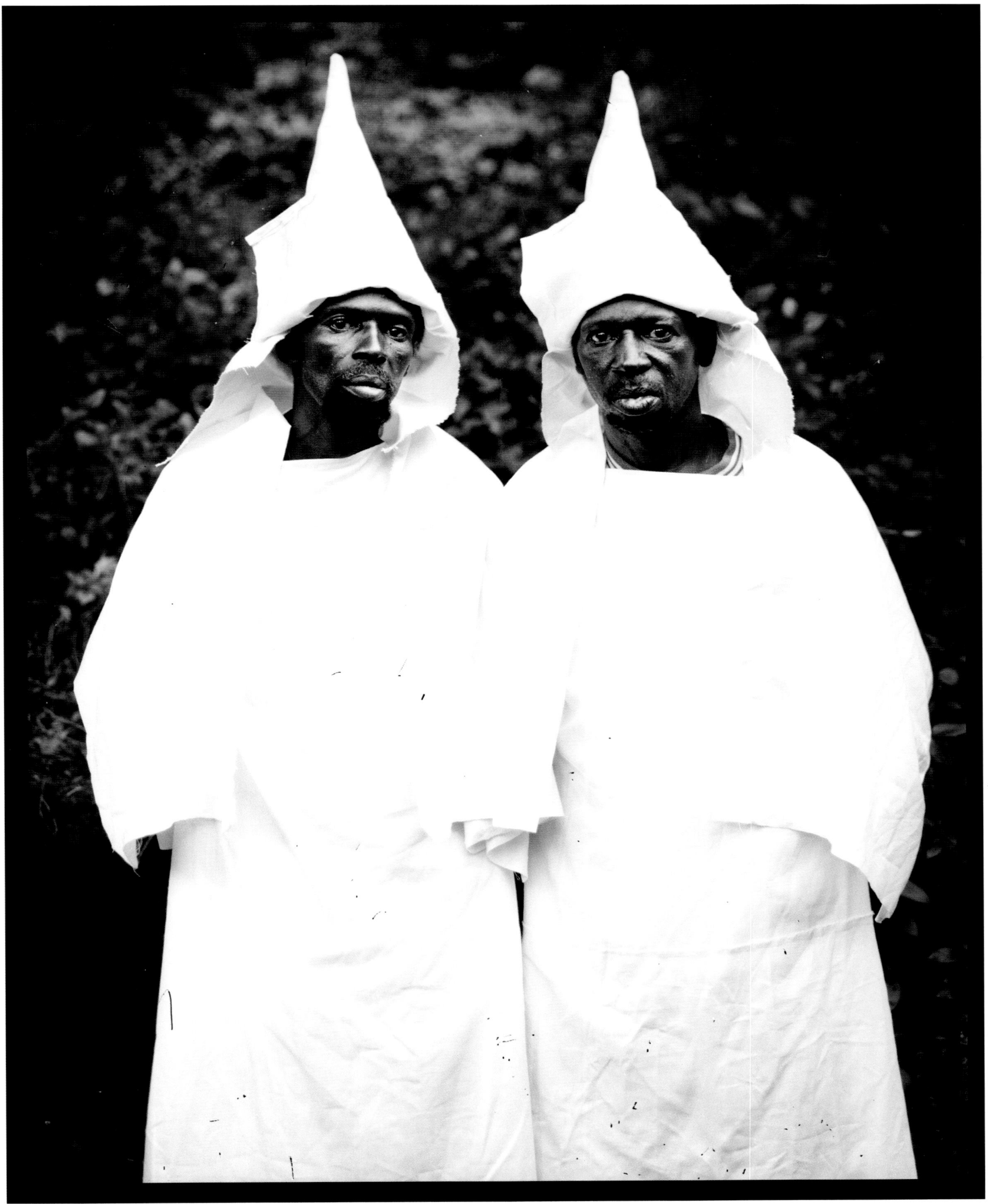

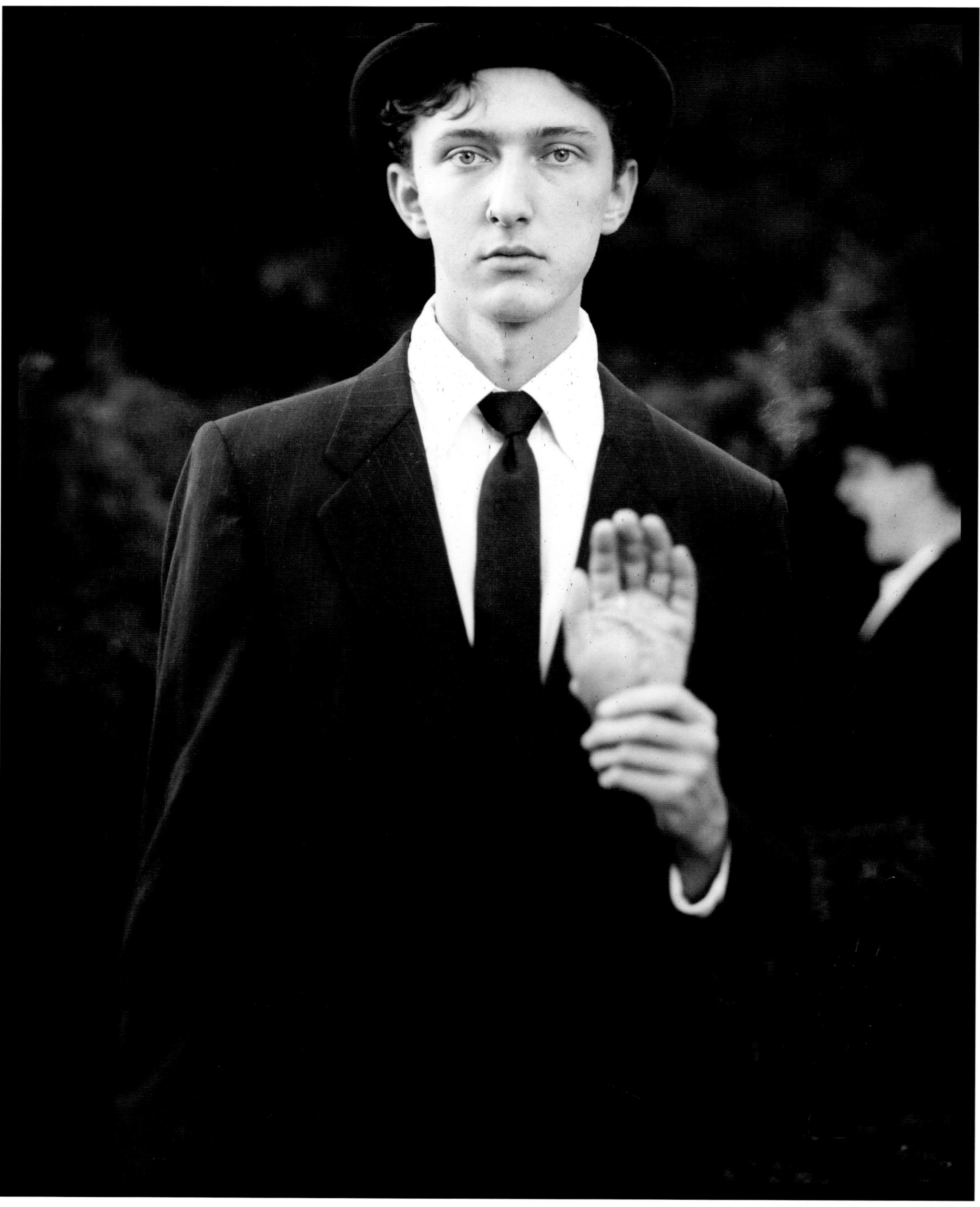

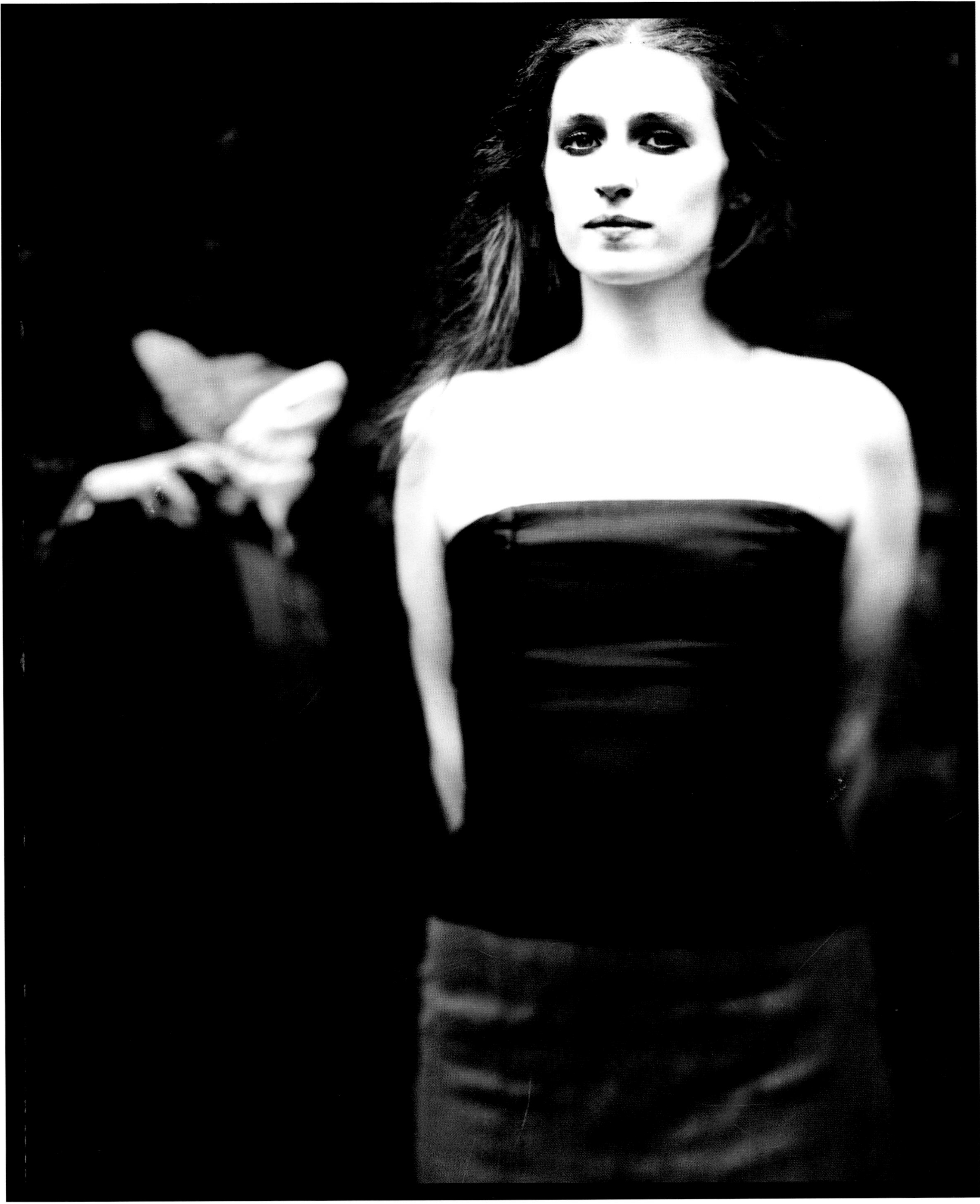

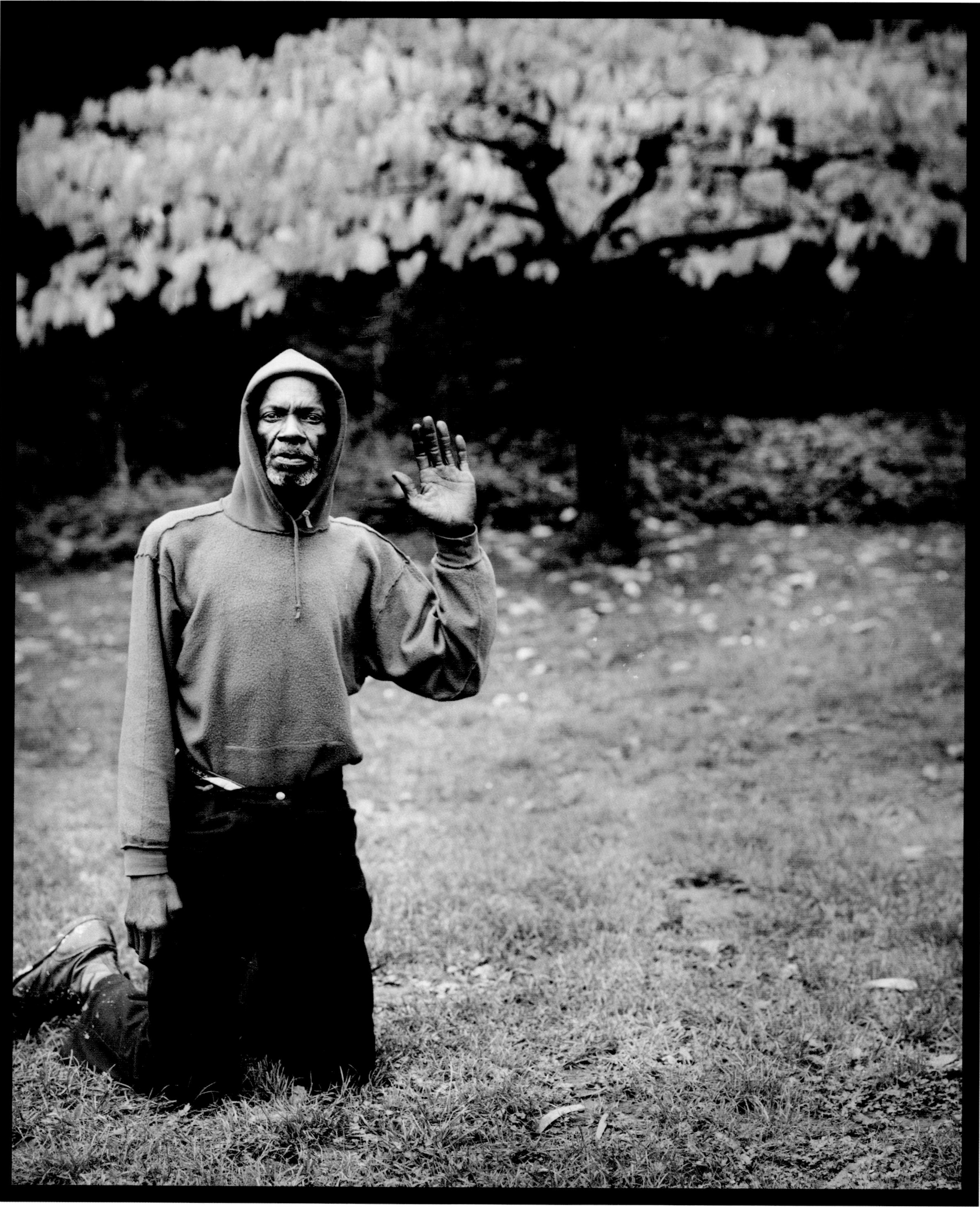

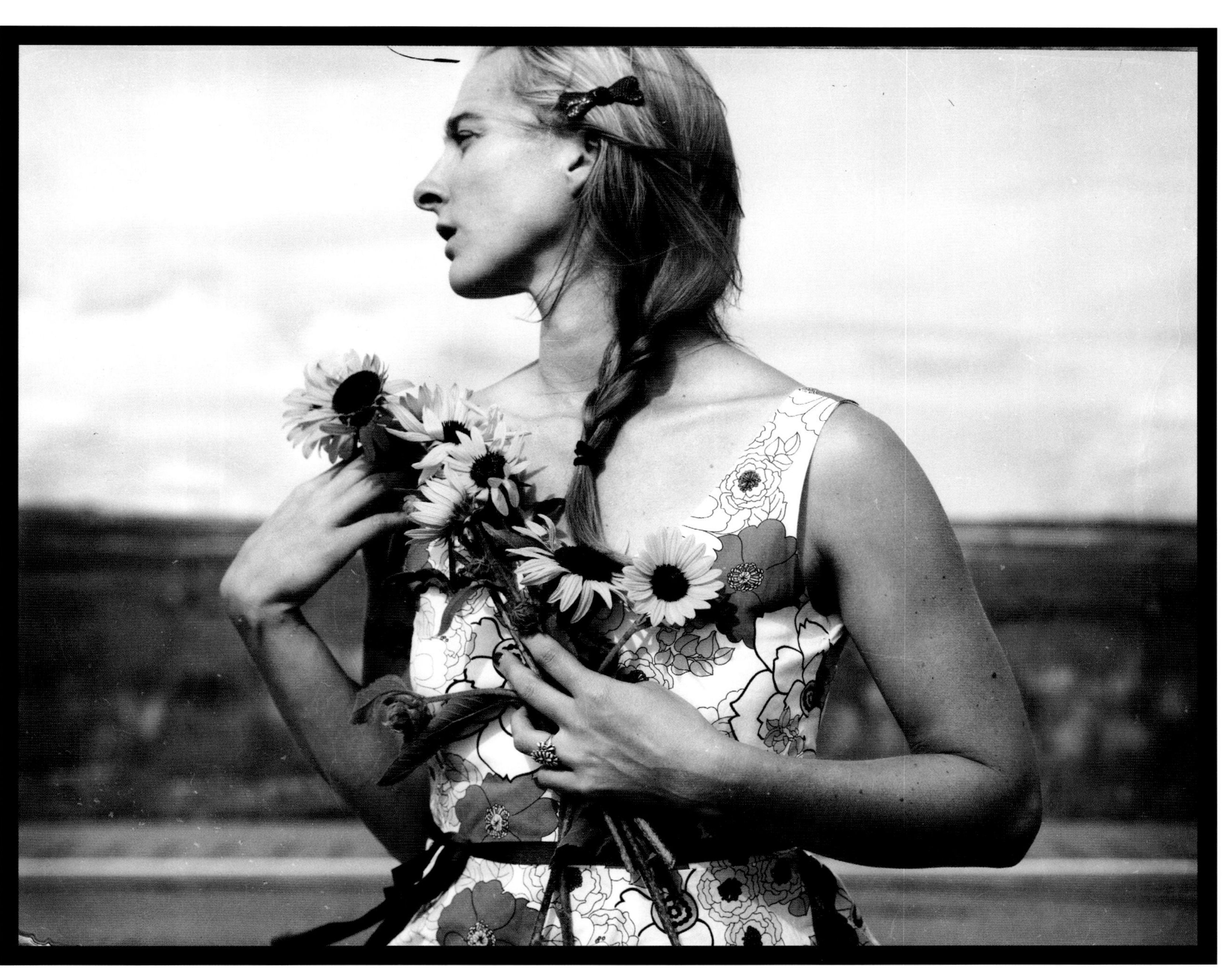

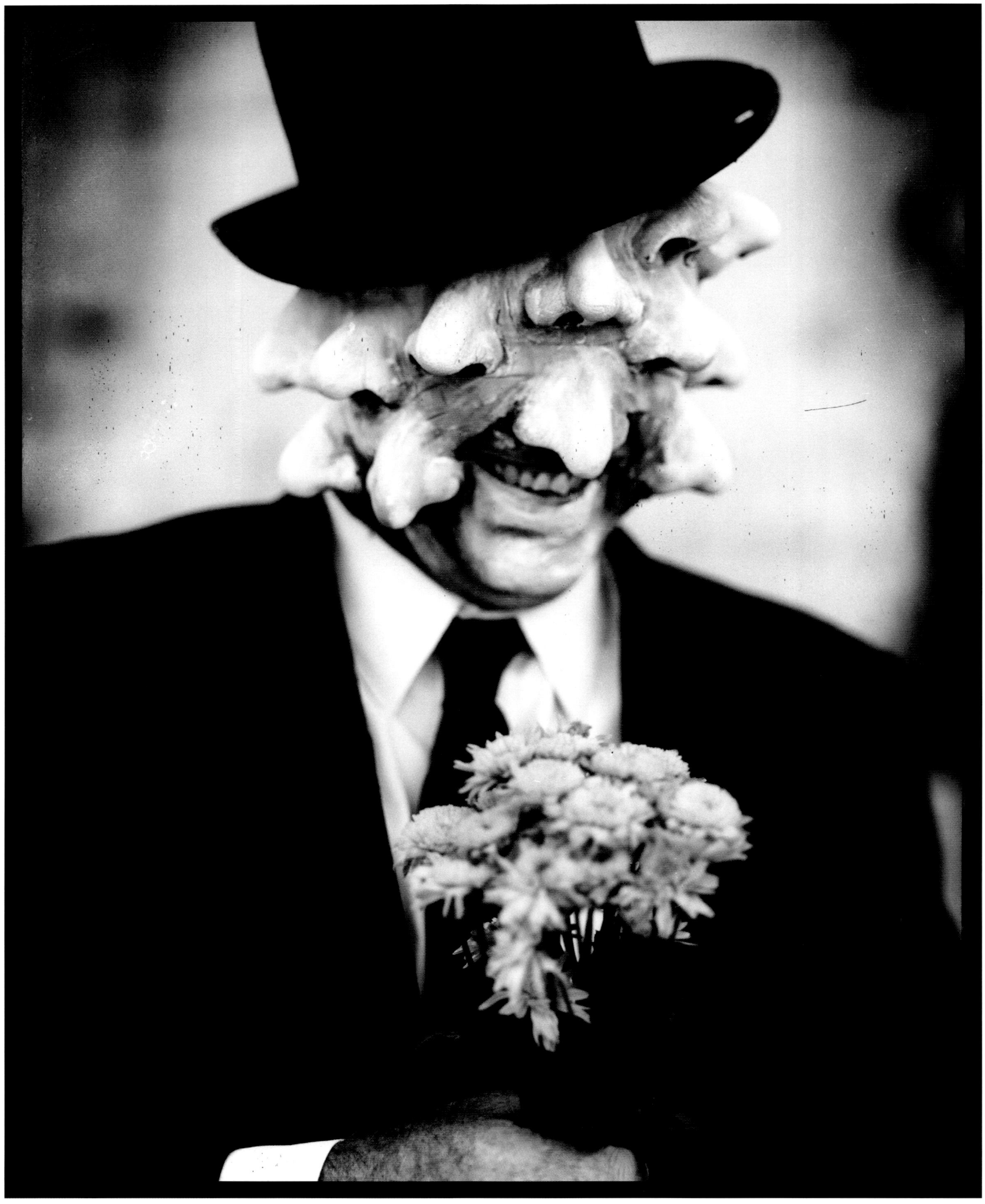

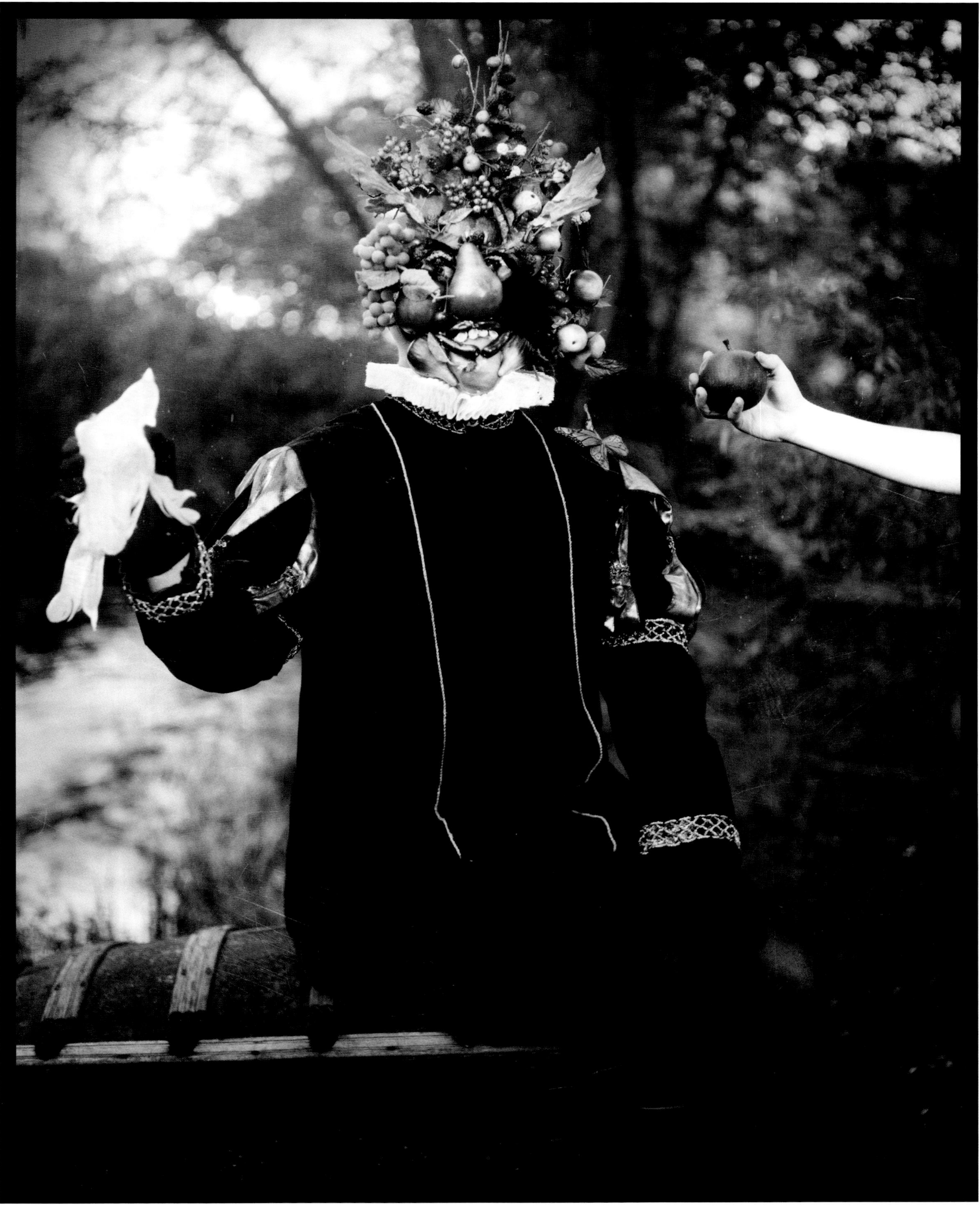

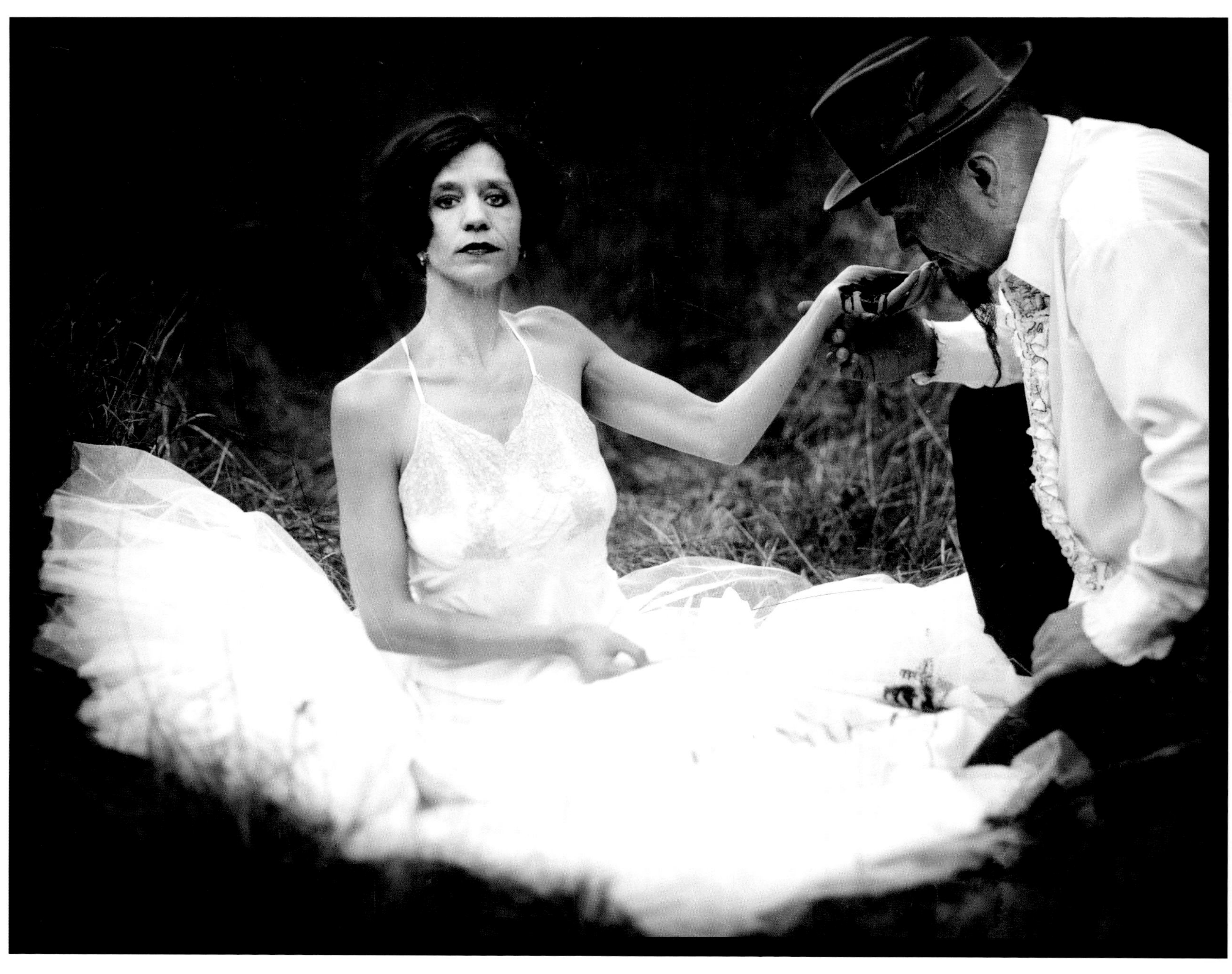

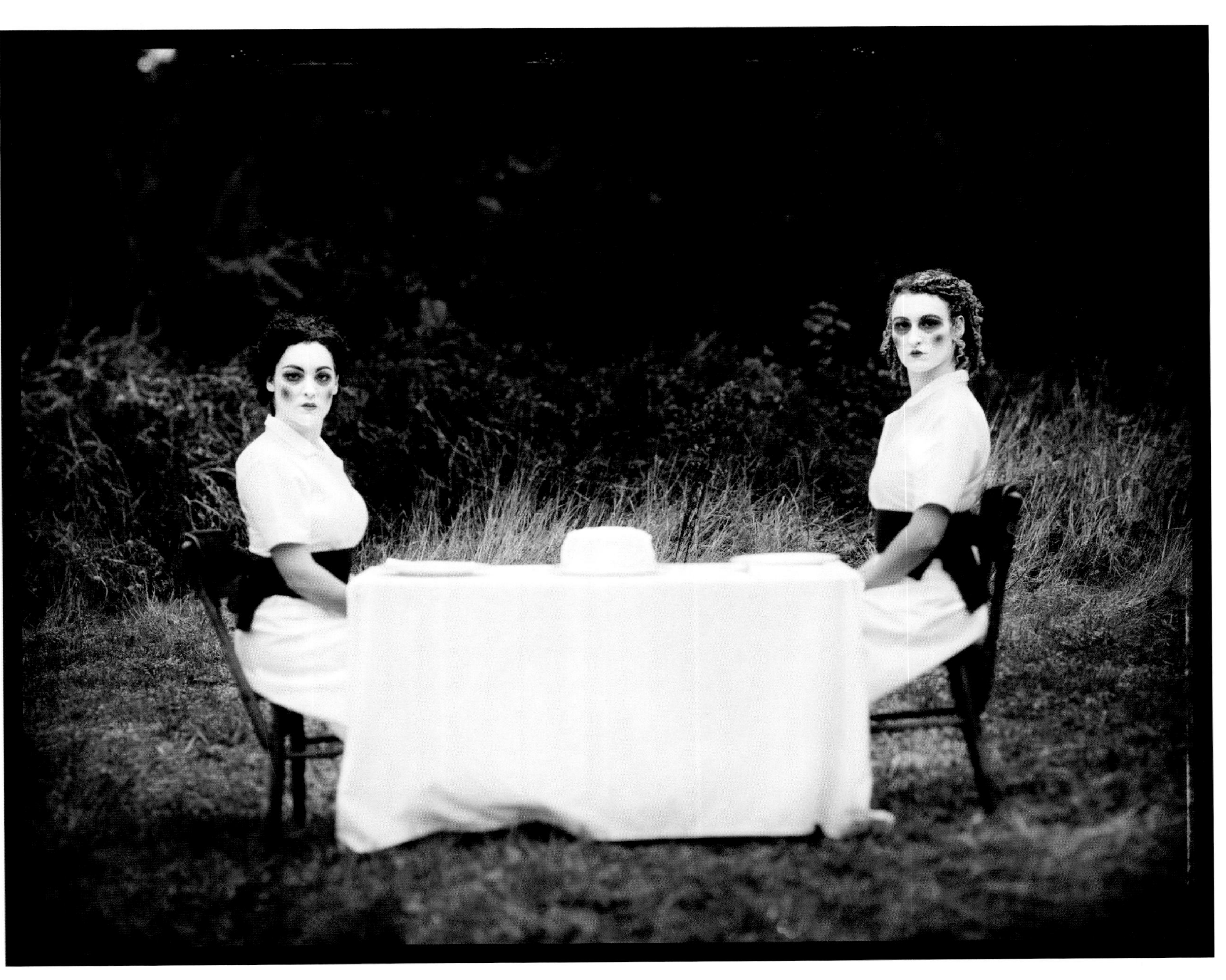

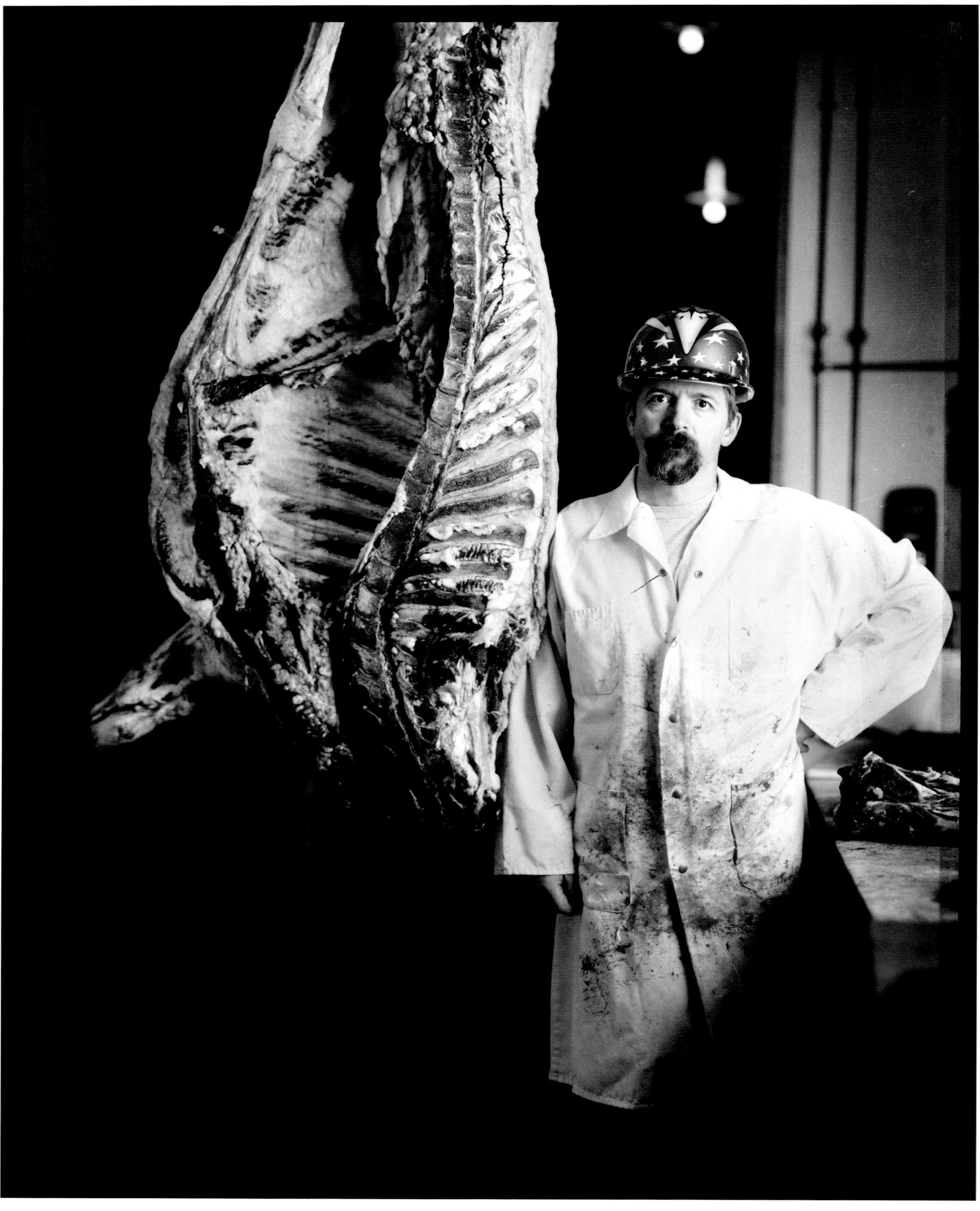

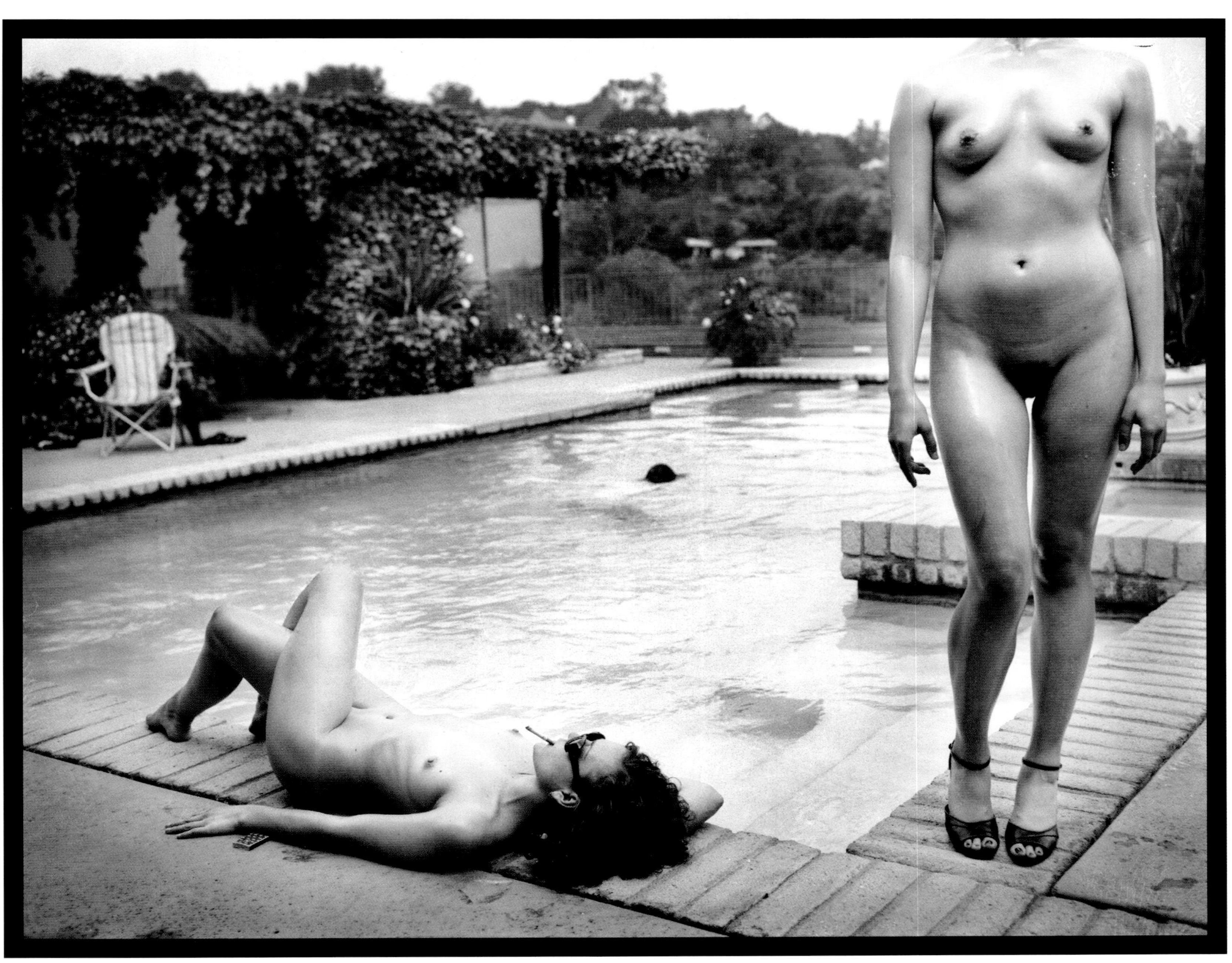

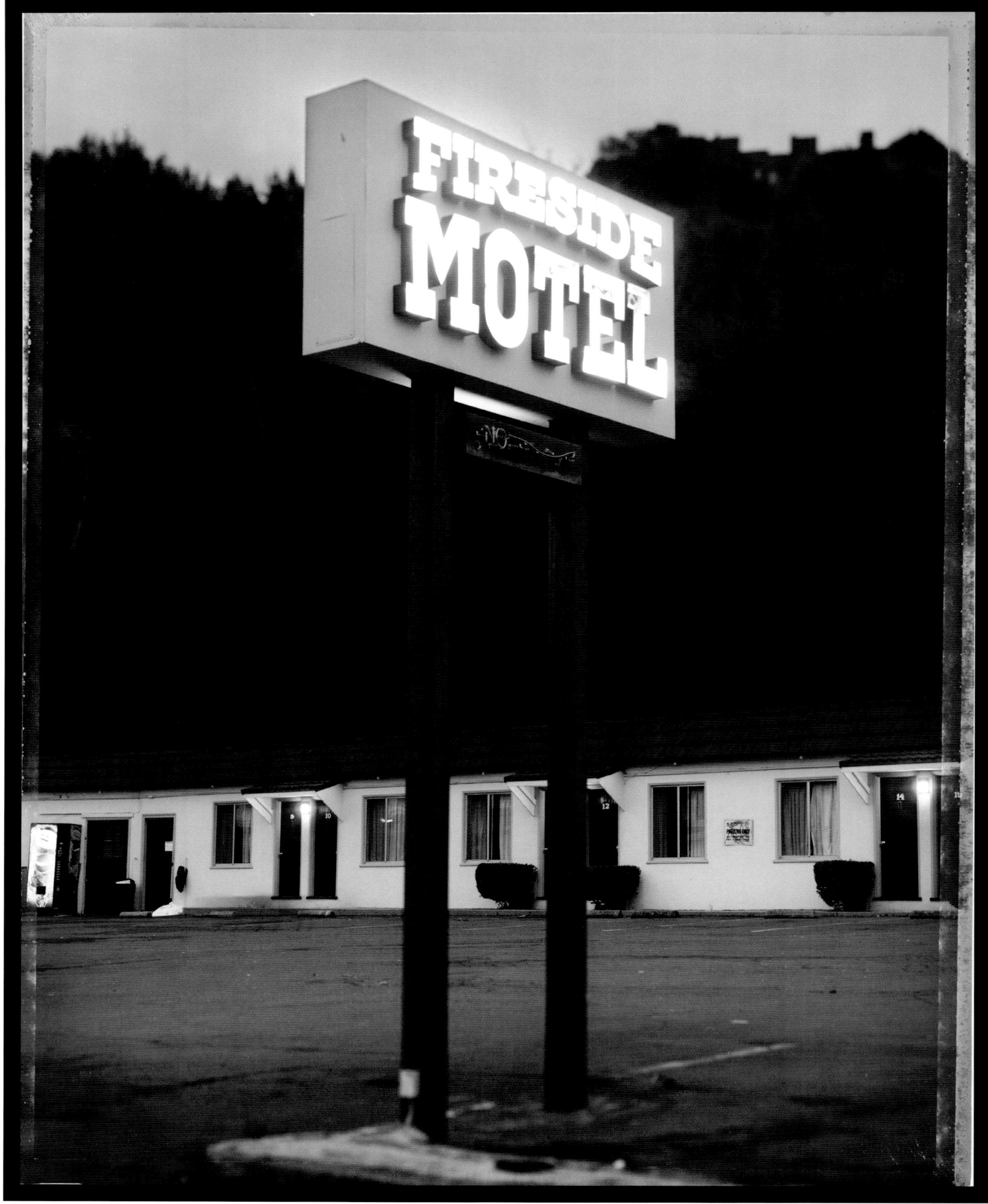
FIRESIDE
MOTEL

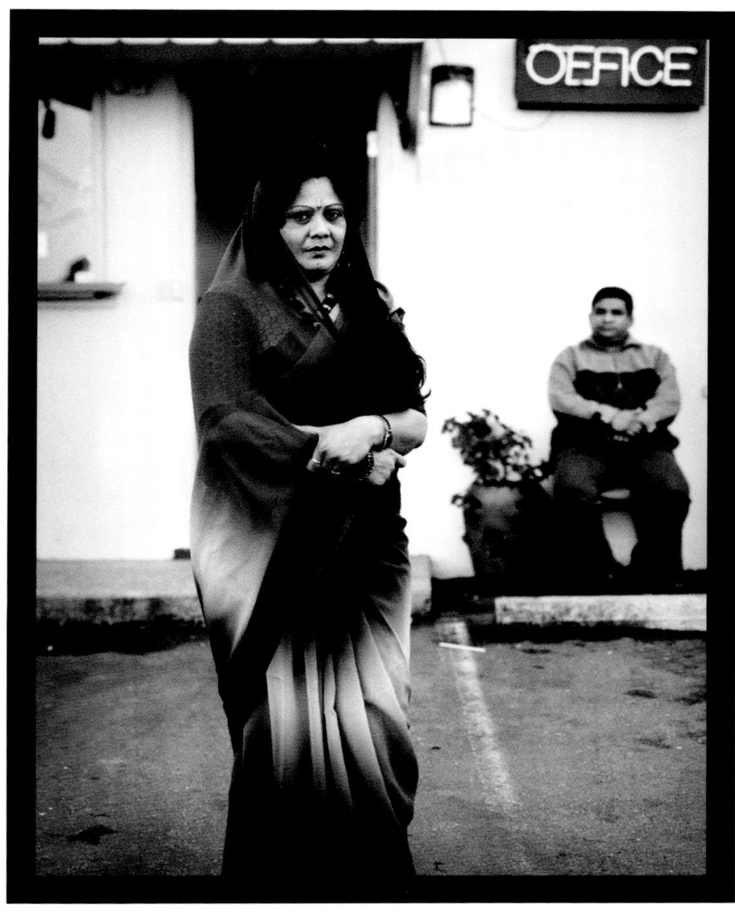
OFFICE

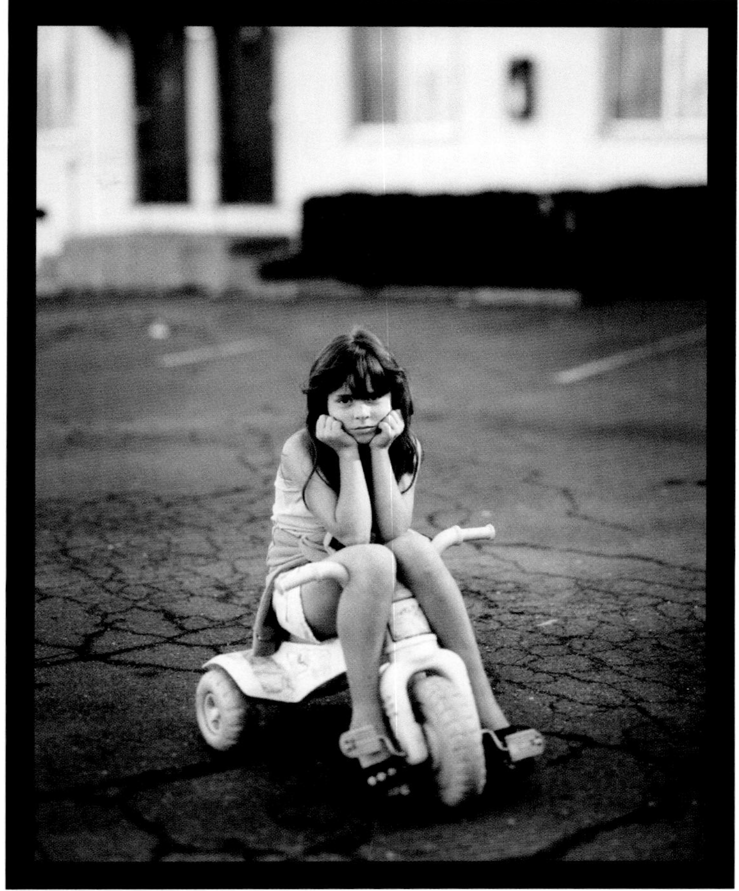

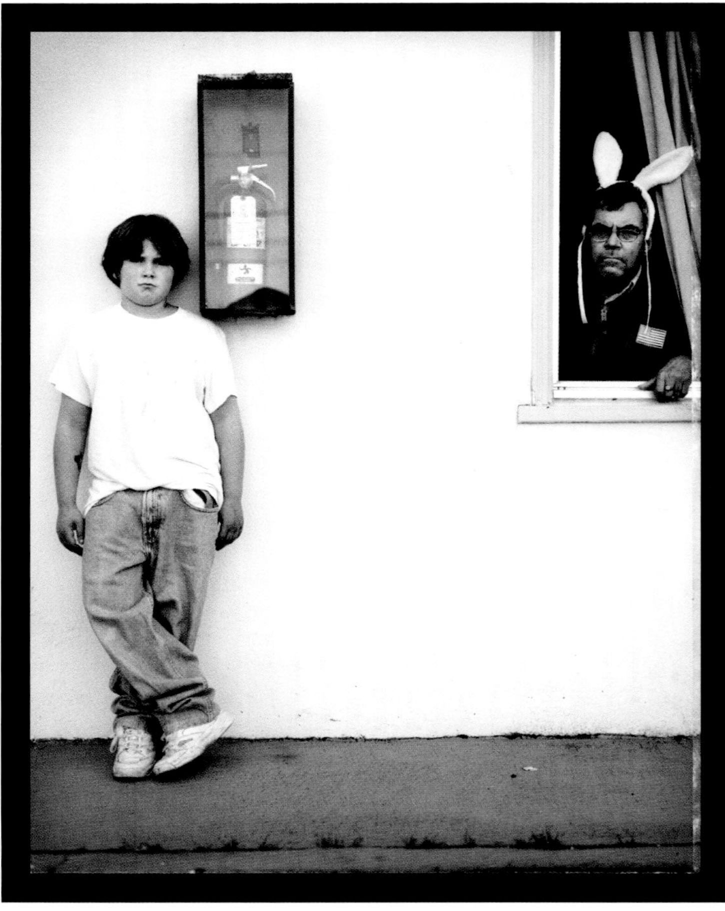

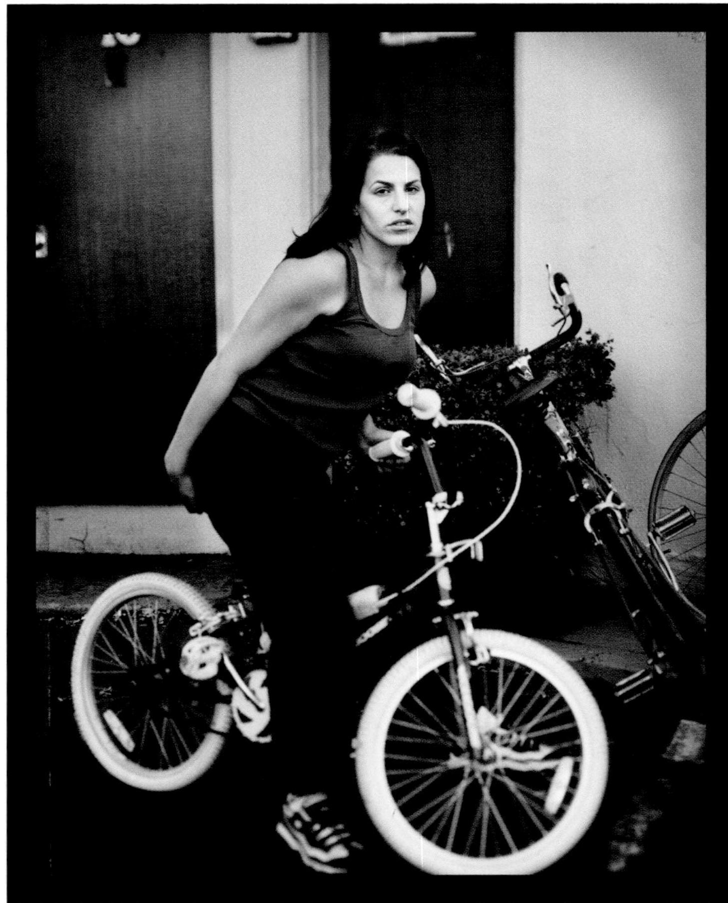

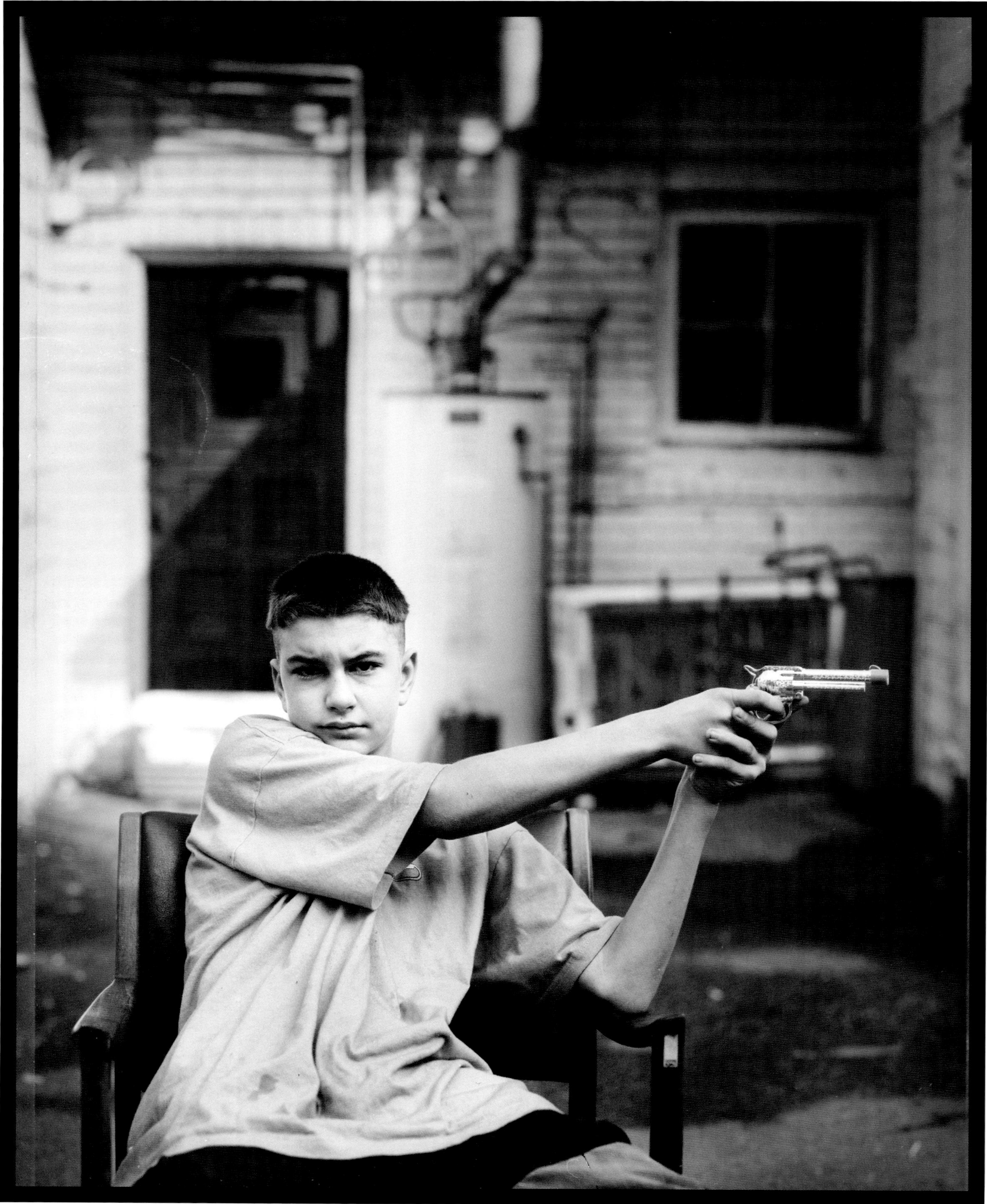

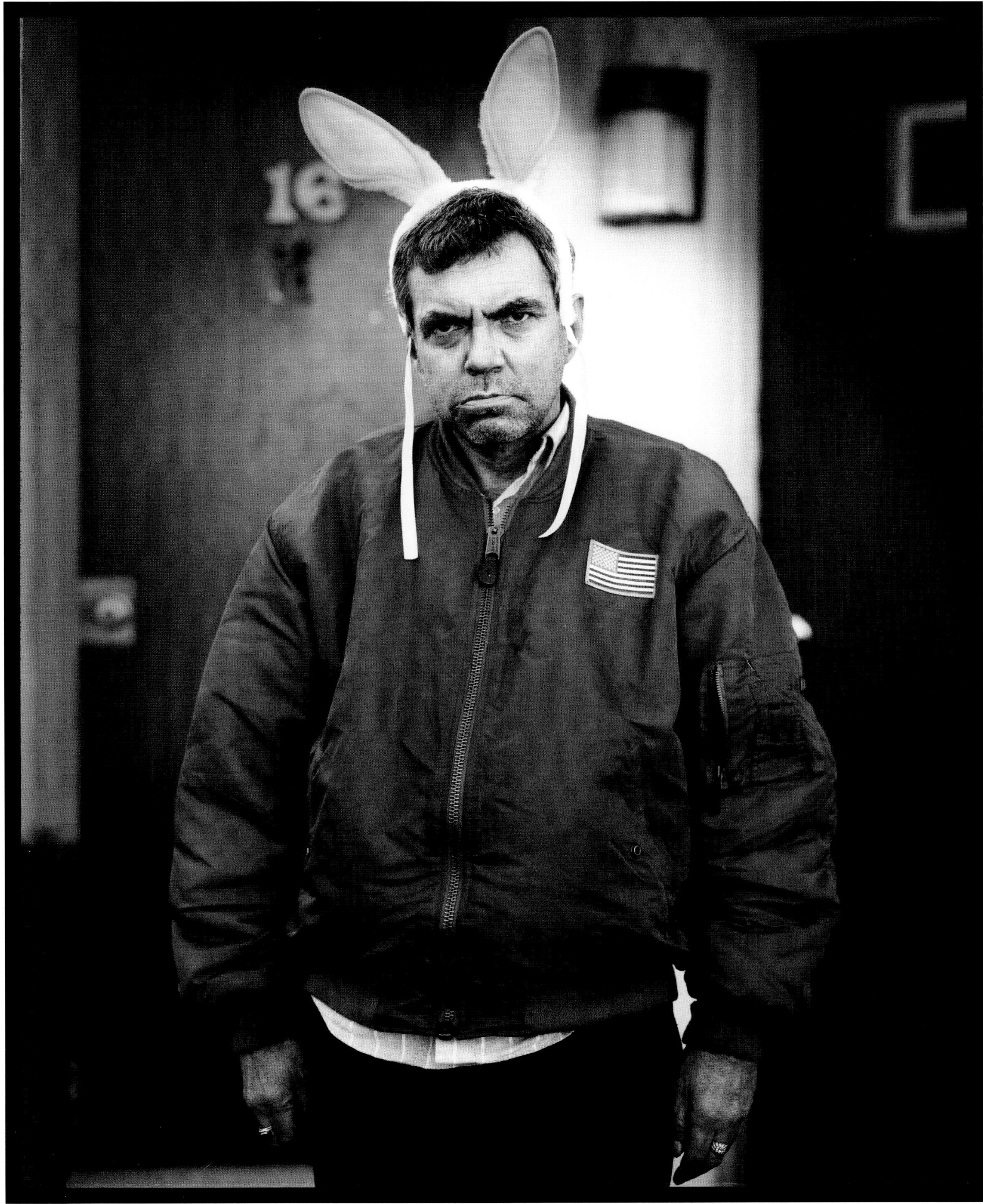
16

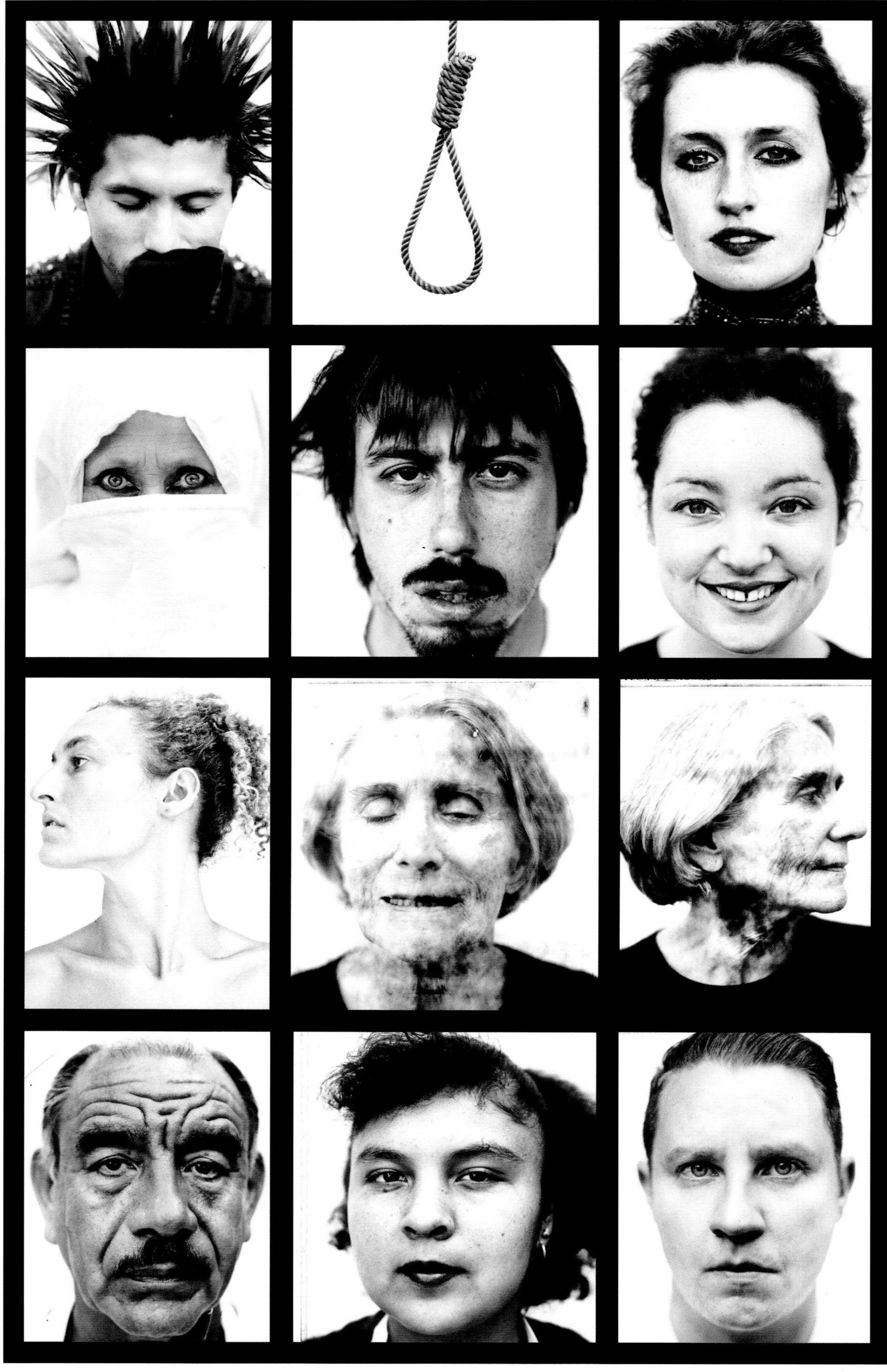

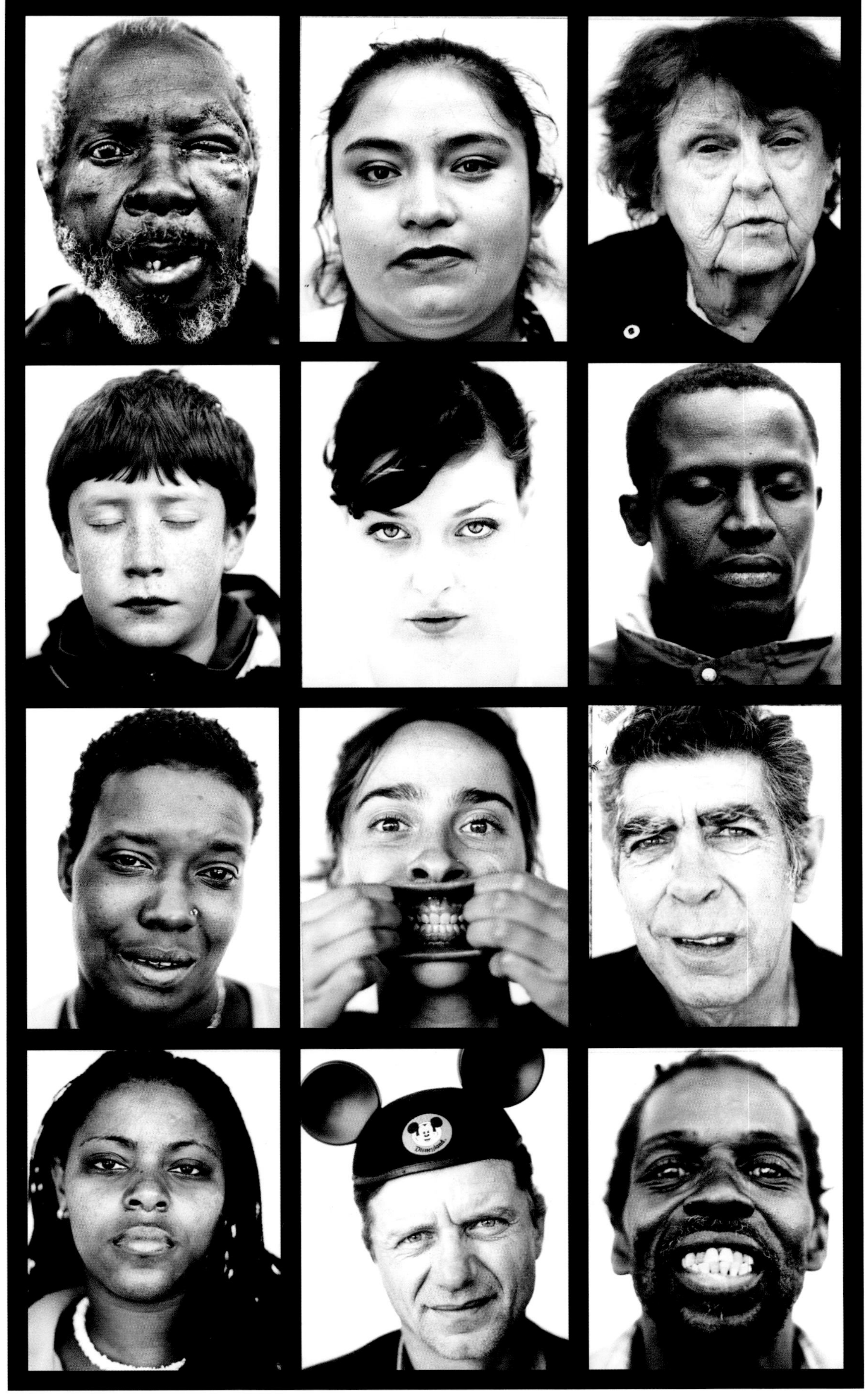
Disneyland

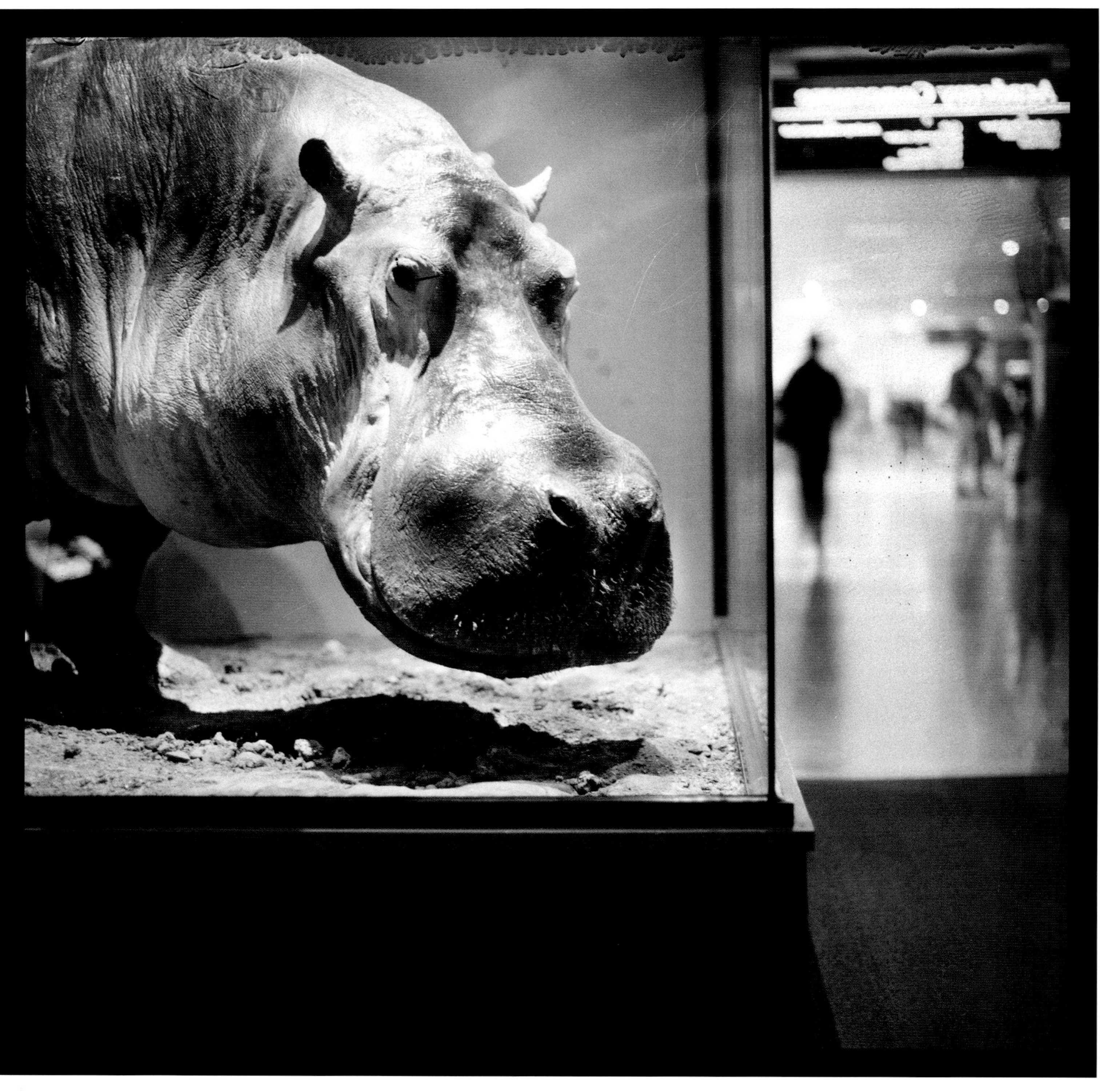

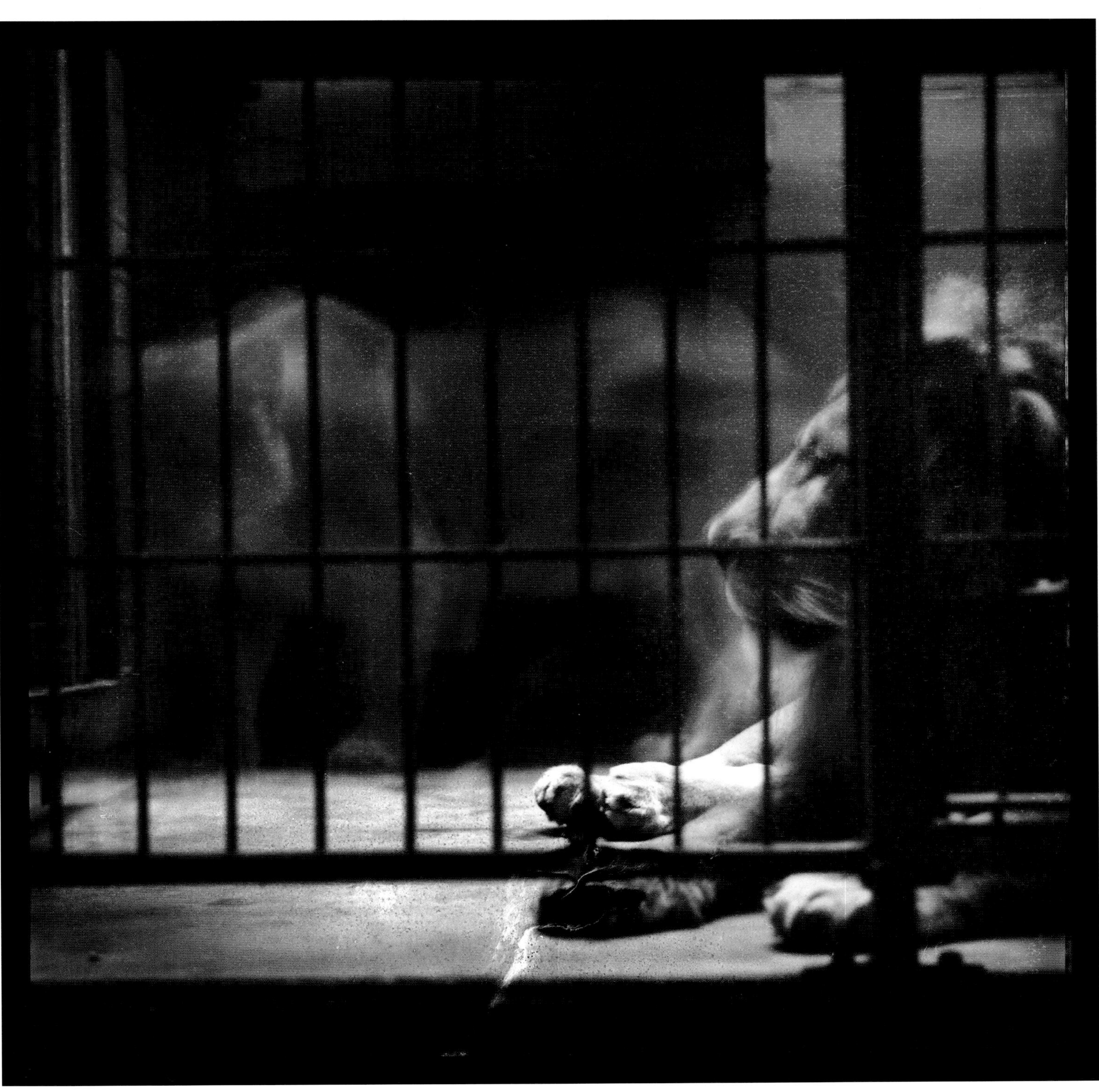

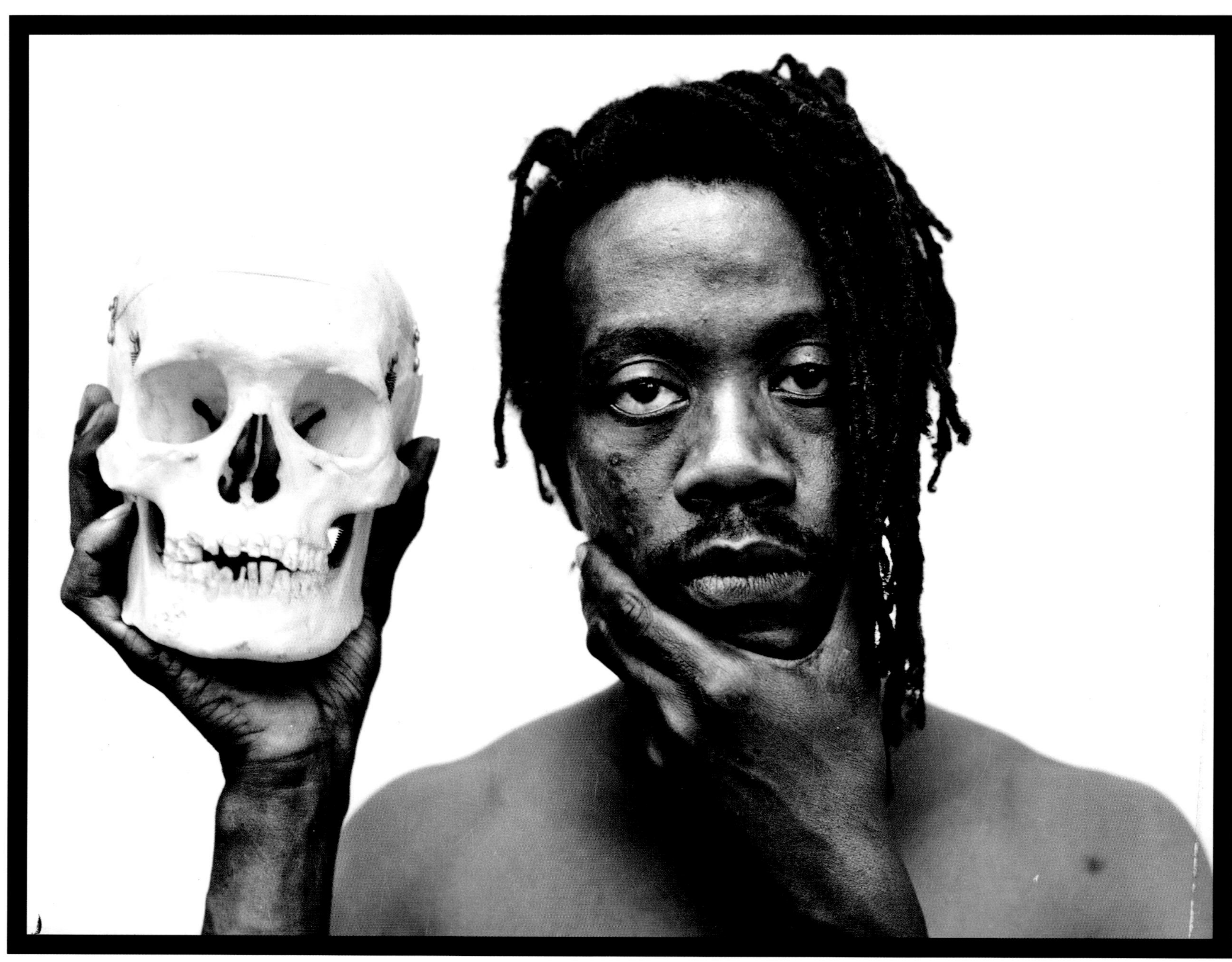

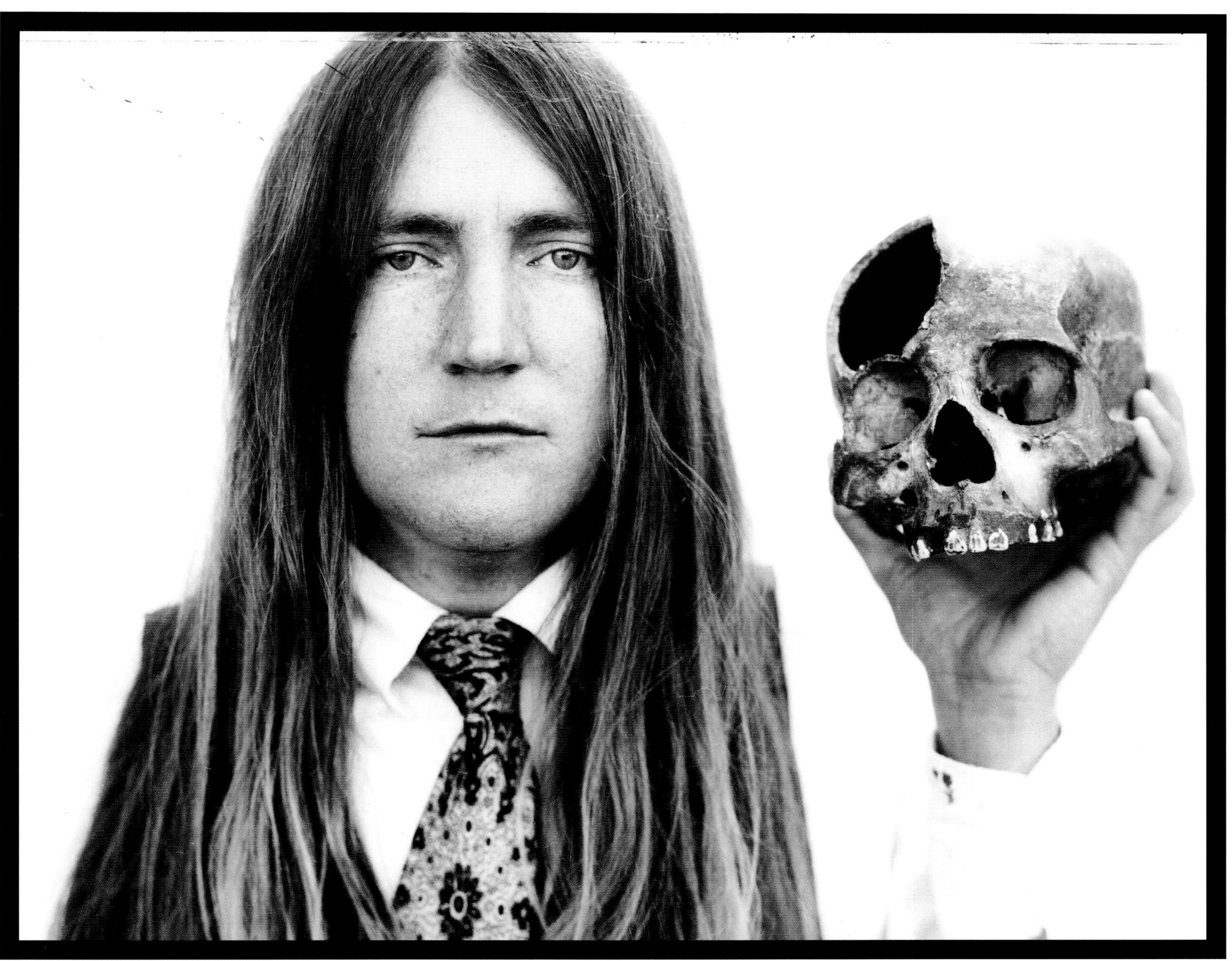

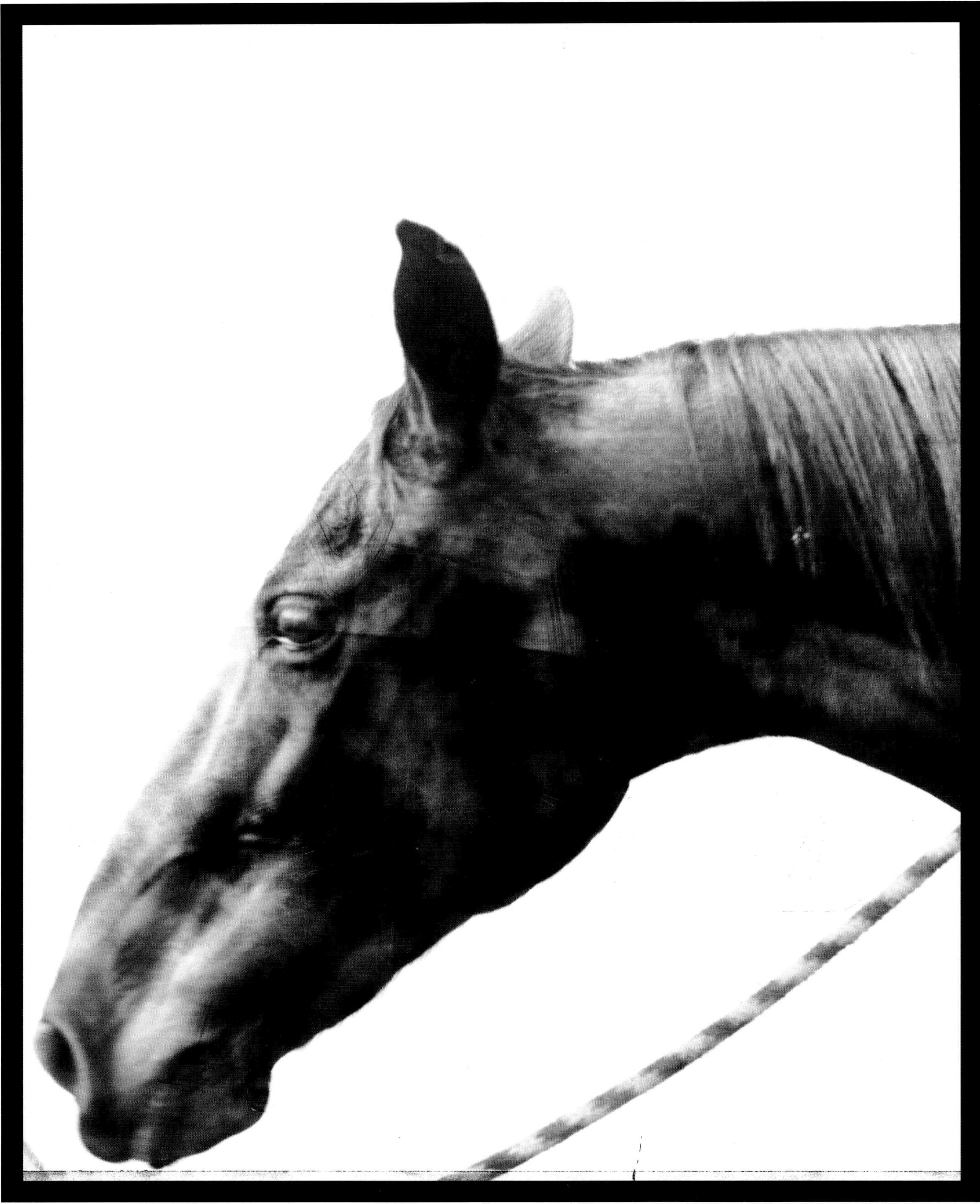

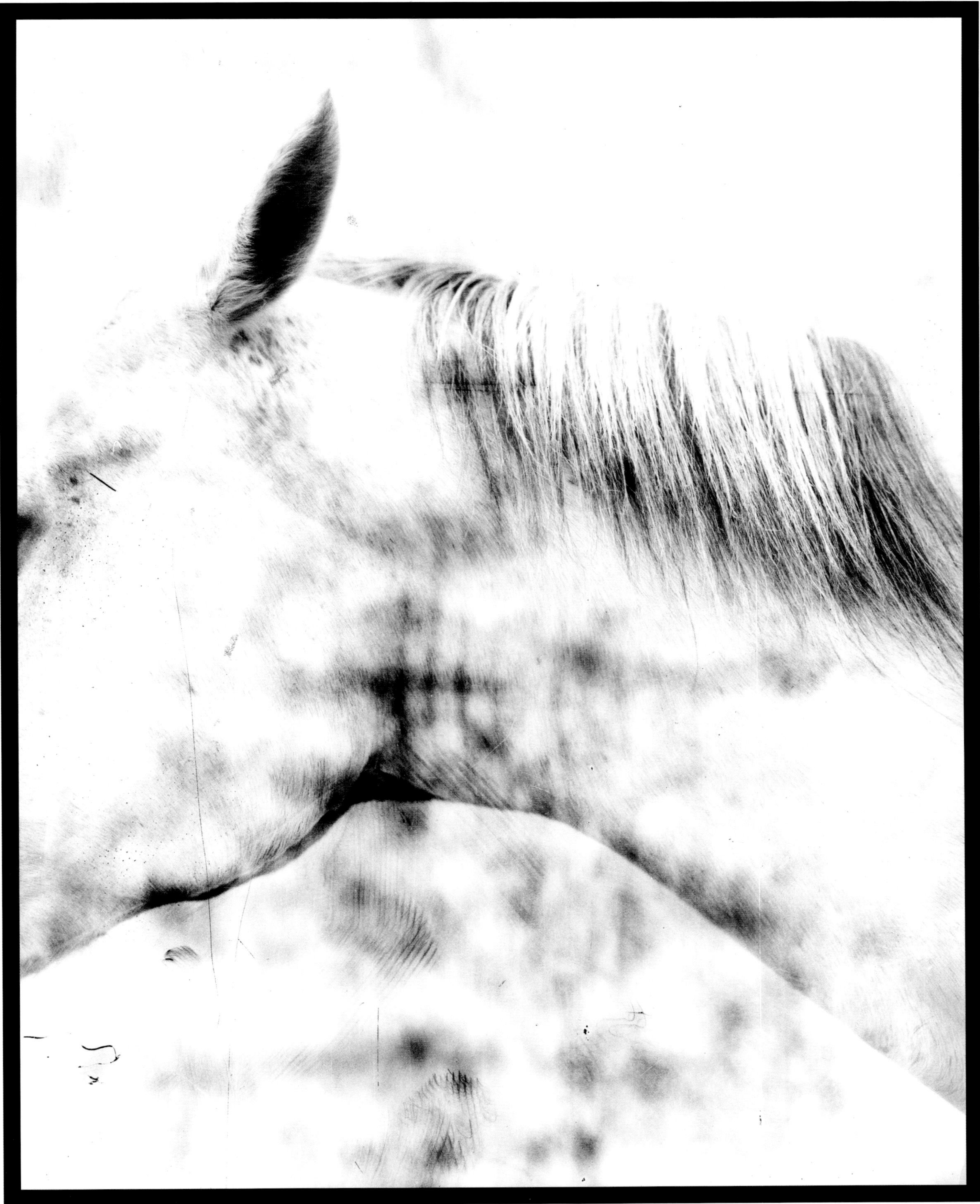

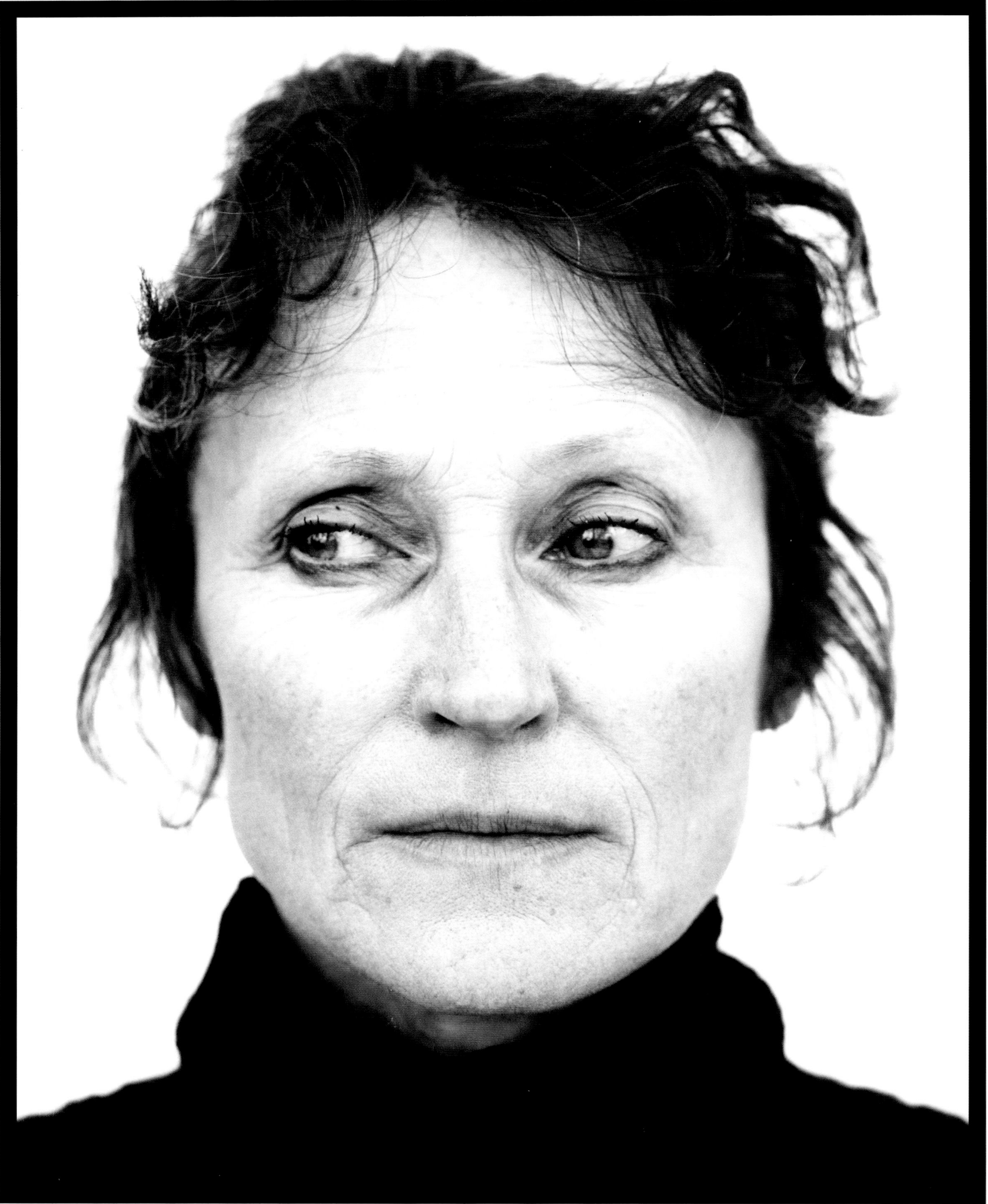

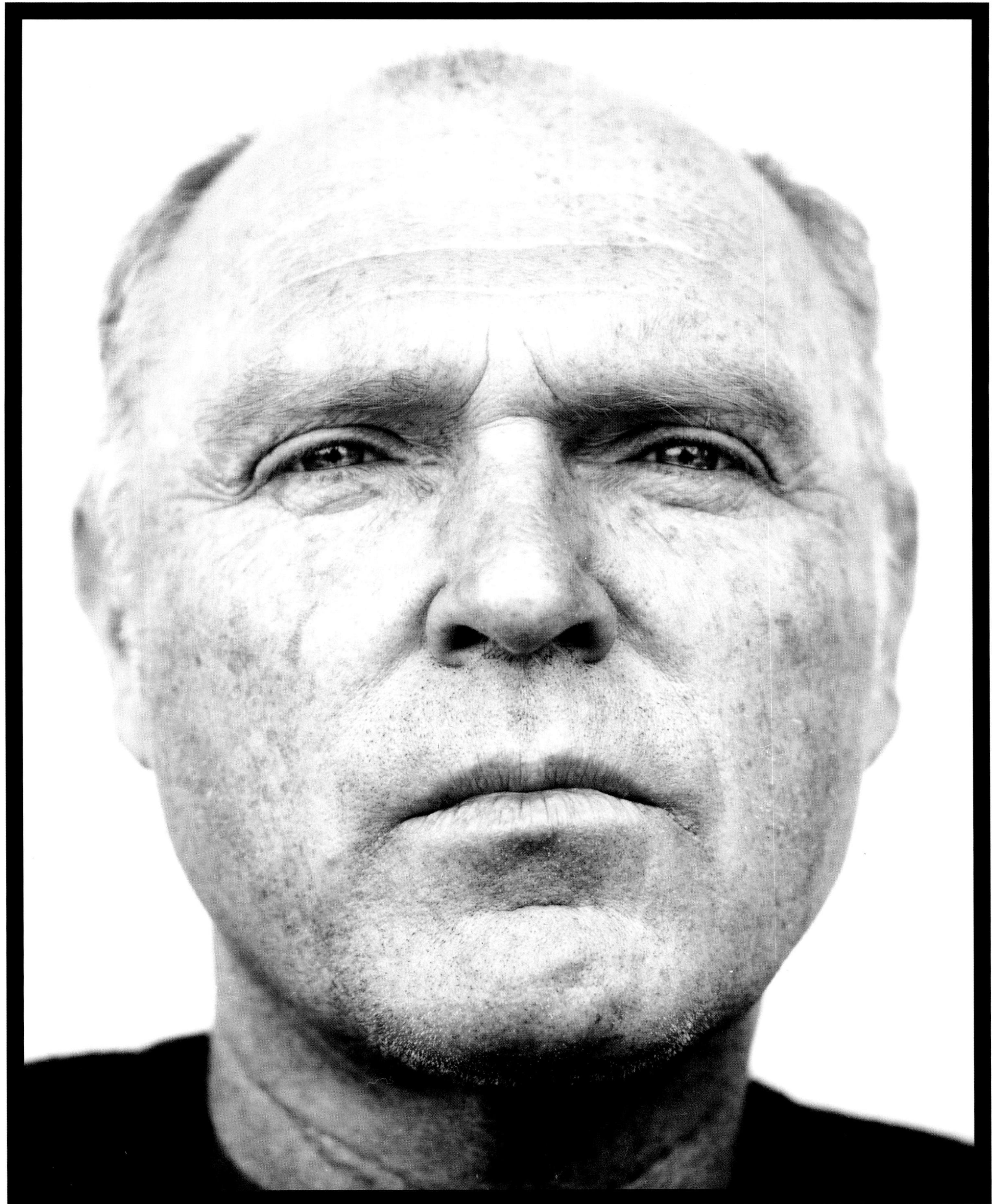

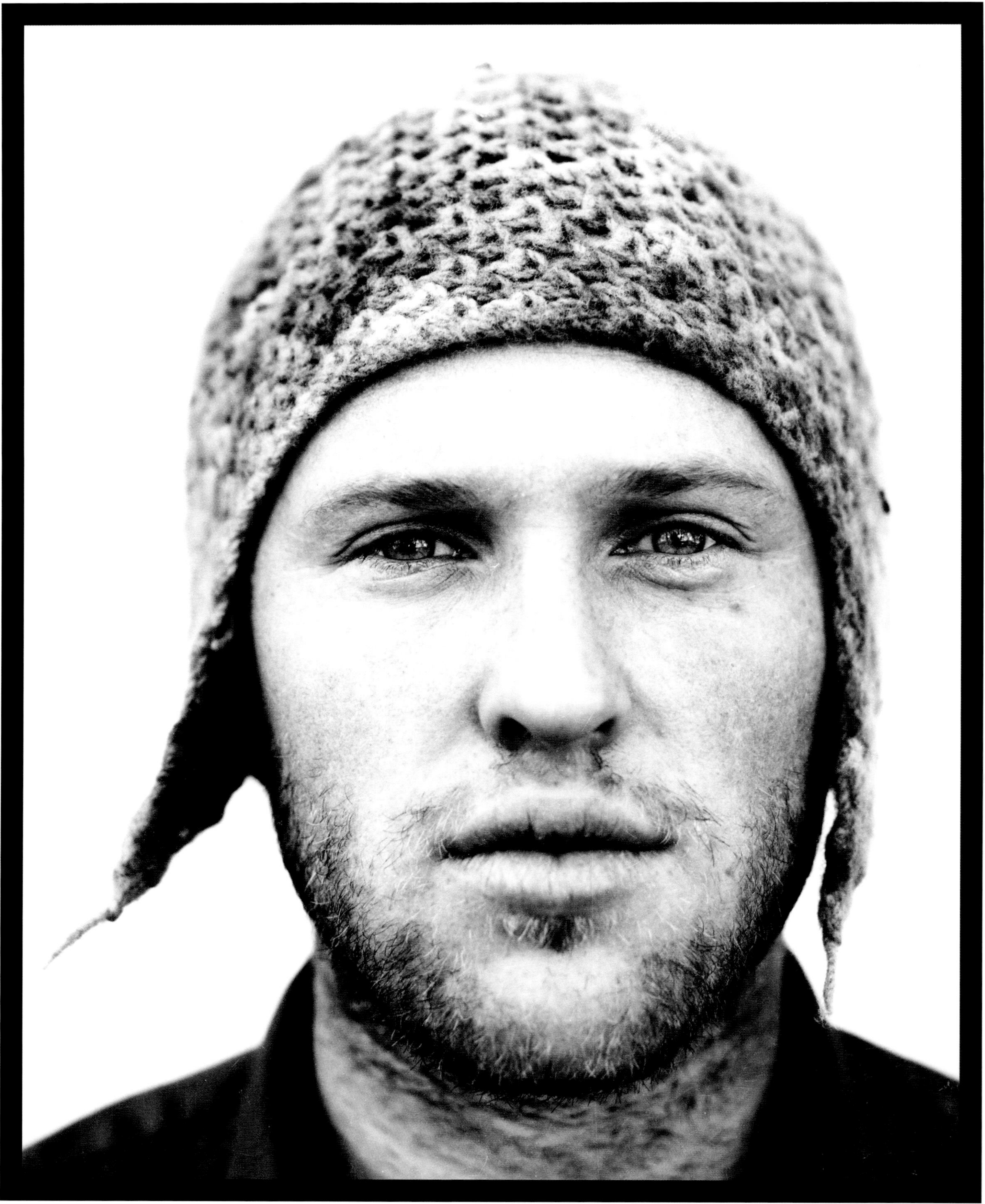

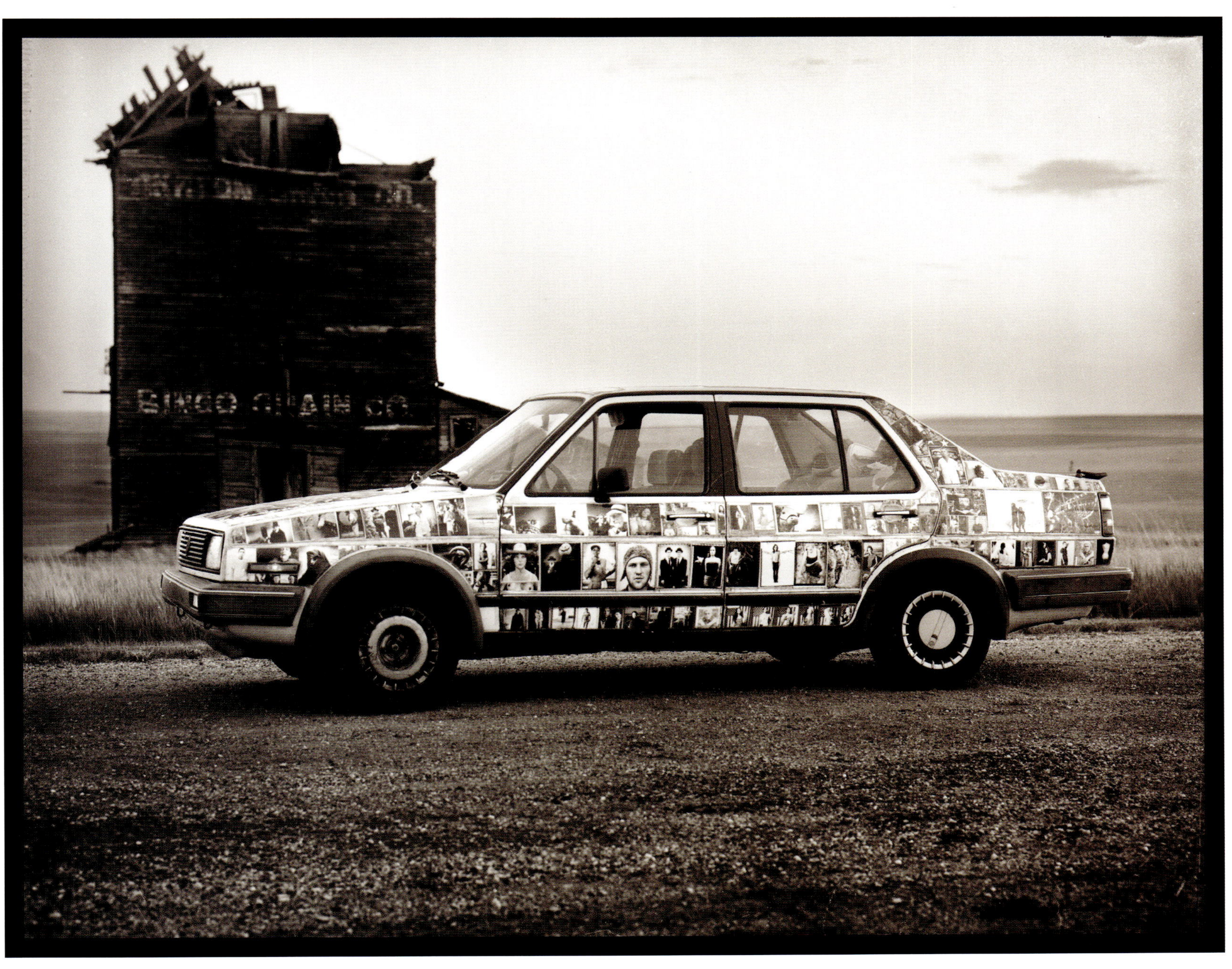
BINGO GRAIN CO.

# Index

Page 5 Nun and Bunny
Page 6 The Daughter of the Circus
Page 7 Praying Monkey
Page 8 The Daughter of the Clown
Page 9 Father Clown
Page 10 Girl in Woods with Animals
Page 11 Girl from Ohio
Page 12 A Bird Flies By
Page 13 Meet Me in Fairfax at 4:30
Page 14 Guadalupe
Page 15 Mishap in the Garden
Page 16 The Gopel Sisters
Page 17 BB Brothers
Page 18 The Virgins
Page 19 4-H Girls
Page 20 Richard and Darth Vader
Page 21 The Swan Rough Draft
Page 22 The Swan
Page 23 Nude in My First Apartment
Page 24 The Lofften Brothers
Page 25 Girl From Montana
Page 26 Elephant Man and Midget
Page 27 Man Waiting for Bus
Page 28 Golden Lords and Lasses
Page 29 The Sunshine Family
Page 30 Le Romance at Motel 6
Page 31 Levitating Girl
Page 32 The Typewriter
Page 33 Foul
Page 34 Girl in the Box 1
Page 35 Girl in the box 2
Page 36 Melina
Page 37 The Apple
Page 38 Mother and Daughter
Page 39 The Pinch
Page 40 The Tunnel 1
Page 41 The Tunnel 2
Page 42 The Family at the Table
Page 43 The Shelter
Page 44 The Check-up
Page 45 Jabberwocky
Page 46 The Fishmonger's Daughter
Page 47 Barbie
Page 48 Daisy in the Pools
Page 49 Little Fish
Page 50 The Ohio Hitchhiker
Page 51 The Flood
Page 52 Lost Lake
Page 53 Dessert Homesteader
Page 54 Dessert Homesteader with the Sire of Man-O-War
Page 55 Dessert Homesteader with Cockatoo
Page 56 Sage Brush Man
Page 57 Nudest Paul
Page 58 Karen with Her New Mohawk
Page 59 Blind Girl
Page 60 Desert Bloom
Page 61 The Family
Page 62 Jerome on the Wrong Road
Page 63 The Rose on the Wrong Road
Page 64 Tin Man
Page 65 The Salesman on the Wrong Road
Page 66 Girl in the Woods
Page 67 Brianna
Page 68 Patriotic Boy
Page 69 Mayor of Blythe
Page 70 Robert, Compton, LA
Page 71 Black Flag
Page 72 Dairy Queen 2
Page 73 Dairy Queen 1
Page 74 Chef and Big Foots
Page 75 Brotherhood Rough Draft
Page 76 Brotherhood 1
Page 77 Brotherhood 2
Page 78 Josh With Hand
Page 79 Taracita
Page 80 Lloyd at the Park, Thanksgiving
Page 81 Girl With Flowers
Page 82 Nose Man
Page 83 The Picker
Page 84 The Feast
Page 85 The Cake
Page 86 Man at the Slaughter House
Page 87 Women at the Pool
Page 88 The Fireside Motel
Page 89 Images from The Fireside Motel
Page 90 Boy with Gun, The Fireside Motel
Page 91 Bunny Man, The Fireside Motel
Page 92 Collage 1
Page 93 Collage 2
Page 94 Hippopotamus at Natural History Museum
Page 95 Lion at Feeding
Page 96 Skull 1
Page 97 Skull 2
Page 98 Black Horse
Page 99 White Horse
Page 100 Mom
Page 101 Dad
Page 102 Mike
Page 103 Photo Car